ANIMAL
HATS

ANIMAL HATS

25

*fun projects
to knit, crochet
or make
from fleece*

RACHEL HENDERSON

with Sarah Kim, Benjamin G. Wilson, Helen Balls,
Charlotte Pyrah, Susan Urquhart and Karen Masters

KYLE BOOKS

First published in Great Britain in 2012 by
Kyle Books
an imprint of Kyle Cathie Ltd.
23 Howland Street
London, W1T 4AY
general.enquiries@kylebooks.com
www.kylebooks.com

ISBN: 978-0-85783-148-4

Text © 2012 Rachel Henderson
Photographs © 2012 Will Heap*
Design © 2012 Kyle Books

* except author photograph on p.6 © Nick Mailer

Designers: Turnbull Grey
Photographer: Will Heap
Editor: Catharine Robertson
Stylist: Ali Allen
Make-up artist: Abbi-Rose Crook
Pattern checkers: Eva Yates and Sarah Kim
Copy editor: Salima Hirani
Proofreader: Katy Denny
Illustrator (for pages 14–39): Roberta Boyce
Production: Nic Jones and Gemma John
Models: Emma Storey, Eleanor Ward, Fiona Rose, Megan
  Orpwood-Russell, Vicky Orchard, Joseph Inniss, Ana Christina
  Grey, Rosie John, Jamie Johnson, Wilfred Johnson, Stanley Heap,
  Scarlett Heap, Tommy Heap

A Cataloguing In Publication record for this title is available from
the British Library.

Printed and bound in China by C&C Offset Printing Company Ltd.

Contents

Knitting, crochet and appliqué are three of my favourite crafts. Since becoming obsessed with these skills I have enjoyed creating projects that introduce an element of fun to the design, and that are easy to make – so you won't get all in a tangle with the projects in this book!

I have loved animal hats since they arrived on the high street. Not only are they so much fun to wear, but making your own is such an enjoyable process! They also make the perfect birthday or Christmas gift. An animal hat can be worn at any age and there are many to choose from in this book. Whether you're a wonder with wool or a novice stitcher, there's more than one project in this book that's suitable for you.

As you work through the projects in this book, you'll be introduced to a variety of knitting, crochet and appliqué techniques. I have also dedicated a whole chapter to getting you started and also show you how to create fun decorations, from embroidery stitches to woolly tassels. My instructions and tips share what I have found works best for me and, hopefully, will provide you with the confidence to start designing your own projects.

The hat designs

I have tried to cover as many animals as possible in this book. As well as creating my own hat designs, I have commissioned a range of projects that I trust you will thoroughly enjoy making. Up and coming young knitwear designer Sarah Kim introduces six brilliant Intarsia designs that are sure to put a smile on your face! Also, five other talented crafters share with you their favourite animal-hat gift idea that they have made for their families and friends.

All of the knitting and crochet projects have been created using gorgeous Rowan yarns. From kid mohair and cashmere to merino and lambswool, these hats are made with yarns that are super soft, so they are extremely comfortable to wear as well as durable. Get stitching!

So whether you'd like to wear a frog, a dog, or even a cheeky monkey, join the trend and start creating animal hats this winter to make your family and friends smile!

Rachel's Intro

1

Getting Started

CHOOSING HOOKS, NEEDLES AND YARN

There are many different types of yarn on the market today, so it can be confusing to know exactly which yarn to choose, taking into account the type of project you are making.

The three factors you should take into account when choosing a yarn are weight (or thickness), composition (what it's made of) and length.

Weight: This is based on the number of plies (or strands) the yarn is made up of. The thinnest yarn is 2-ply and yarn goes up in size through 3-ply, 4-ply, double knit (DK), aran, and chunky to super-chunky.

Composition: Yarns are made up of many different fibres, from natural ones such as merino wool, alpaca, silk, cotton and linen to man-made ones such as nylon, acrylic and viscose. The yarn's ball band will always tell you what the yarn is made of and also provide washing instructions.

Length: The metreage of yarn in a ball can vary, even if the yarns are of the same type and the balls weigh the same. It is the metreage that is vital, so if you are substituting a yarn, check the ball band for the metreage and ensure you buy enough.

Like yarn, knitting needles and crochet hooks also come in various materials – metal, plastic, bamboo and wood. All of them will give the same results, but some people prefer bamboo knitting needles over metal or plastic ones because they are lighter and can be easier to work with. Likewise, aluminium crochet hooks are popular as they often have a strong plastic shaft which is easy to grip and lighter on your fingers. At the end of the day, go with what works best for you.

A knitting or crochet pattern will always tell you what type of yarn to use and what size needles or hook to use. If you want to choose a different yarn from that suggested, the important thing to do is to match the tension of that yarn to the one given in the pattern. A suggested tension will usually be shown on a yarn's ball band.

Yarns

1. Super chunky pure merino wool

2. Merino wool and kid mohair chunky yarn

3. Aran weight wool and alpaca mix

4. Baby alpaca and merino wool mix

5. Lambswool and kid mohair mix

6. 100 per cent baby alpaca dk yarn

7. 100 per cent cotton spring/summer yarn

8. Merino wool and cotton mix yarn

Equipment

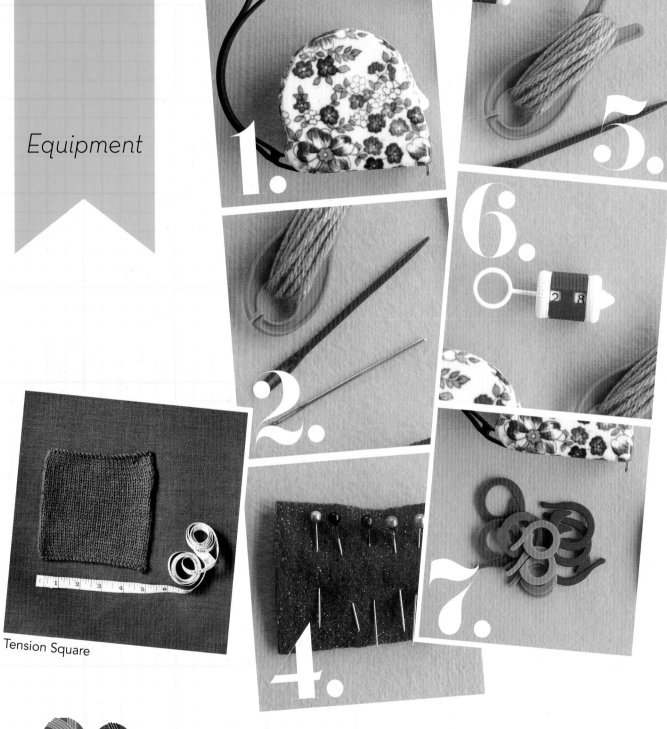

1.

2.

4.

5.

6.

7.

Tension Square

Equipment

To be honest, when you are knitting or crocheting, all you really need is a pair of needles or a crochet hook and some yarn but, as with anything, you can buy as much or as little equipment as you like. The items below will help your knitting and crocheting go smoothly.

1. Tape measure: This is a vital thing to have, especially when checking your tension square at the beginning of a project.

2. Darning needles: These are essential for darning in ends and sewing up your project. If you are using a very chunky yarn, ensure it will fit through the eye of your needle.

3. Scissors: A small pair of scissors is always useful for trimming the ends of yarns.

4. Pins: When you are sewing up your project, use pins to keep the fabric in place.

5. Bobbins: These are really handy to have when working on a project with different coloured yarns. They help to keep the yarns from tangling and speed up the process of knitting with different colours.

6. Stitch counter: Hang one on the end of one of your knitting needles to help you keep count of what row you are on.

7. Crochet markers: These help to identify the start of a round, which is very handy when you are making hats!

Tension

You will always hear the word 'tension' in a conversation about knitting and crochet, but what does it mean?

Your tension is how tightly or loosely you knit or crochet. Most people don't realise how important it is to get it right until they begin their first project, but it will affect the size of your finished garment or accessory. If you knit or crochet tightly, your project might end up too small; if you knit or crochet loosely, it might end up too big.

Always make a tension square before you start a project to find out if you should be using the size of needles/hook suggested in the pattern. The pattern you are working from will tell you how many stitches and rows you should have to produce a 10cm/4in square of knitted fabric. When making your tension swatch always cast on/chain at least 6 more stitches than the number given and knit/crochet at least 6 more rows. If you don't do this your tension square might end up smaller than 10cm, making it difficult to count how many rows and stitches you have.

Measuring your tension square
Lay the square on a flat surface. To count the stitches, lay a tape measure horizontally across the square, with the end a couple of stitches in from the edge, and count the number of stitches to 10cm/4in. To count the rows, do the same thing but lay the tape vertically down the square.

If you have too many stitches, go up a needle/hook size to the one stated in the pattern. If you have too few stitches, use a smaller needle/hook to the one stated in the pattern.

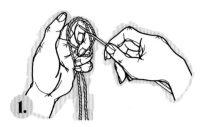

KNITTING

1. Basic techniques
(how to cast on and off)

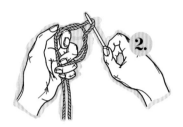

How to cast on

This is where it all starts. Casting on is how you get the right number of stitches onto your needle to begin your project.

Don't pull on the yarn too hard or your cast-on stitches will be too tight, making it difficult to knit the first row.

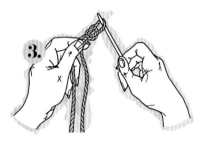

Knitted cast on

This method of casting on provides a firm, strong edging for a piece of knitted fabric, and works well with stocking stitch.

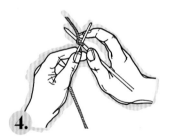

1. Before you cast on your stitches, leave a short tail of yarn and make a slip knot by winding the yarn twice around 2 fingers on your left hand, with the second loop behind the first.

2. Hold a knitting needle in your right hand and use the tip to pull the second loop of yarn through the first loop on your fingers.

3. Pull both ends of the yarn to tighten the knot. You now have your first cast-on stitch. Hold this needle in your left hand and its partner in your right hand.

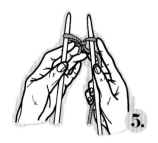

4. Insert the right needle up through the bottom of the stitch on the left needle and to the back of the left needle, making a cross with the needles. Then wrap the working yarn around the right needle, taking it behind the right needle and around it to bring it forwards between both needles.

5. Slide the right needle down through the top of the slip knot on the left needle and under towards the front of the left needle, pulling the yarn you wrapped around it through the loop. You should now have a loop on each needle.

6. Slip the loop on the right needle onto the left needle and gently pull the yarn tight. You should now have 2 stitches on the left needle. Working into the first stitch (the one nearest the tip) on the left needle, repeat steps 4–6 until you have the required number of cast-on stitches.

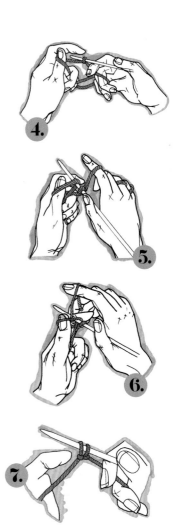

Thumb method

Also known as long-tail cast on, this method provides a more elastic edging to a piece of knitted fabric, and is ideal when working in garter stitch.

First, follow steps 1–3 of the Knitted Cast On (see opposite), leaving a long yarn tail. You are going to use the long tail to cast on all your stitches.

4. Hold the knitting needle with the slip knot in your right hand along with the working yarn. Hold your tail yarn in the last 3 fingers of your left hand, so that it is stretched between the needle and the left hand. Your thumb should be pointing upwards. From this position, twist your thumb backwards, moving it back over the outstretched tail yarn, then down and under it to catch it, then towards the front and back to pointing upwards, now with the yarn looped around it.

5. Insert the right needle into the bottom of the thumb loop.

6. Take the working yarn around the back of the needle, then pass it between the needle and the thumb, towards the front. Lift the thumb loop over the tip of the needle.

7. Pull the tail yarn tight. You should now have 2 cast-on stitches on your needle. Repeat steps 4–7 until you have the required number of cast-on stitches on your needle.

How to cast off

Casting off is a very simple process and is done after you have finished your piece of knitting to secure your stitches so they don't unravel.

1. First of all, you need to knit 2 stitches.

2. Using the left needle, pick up the first knitted stitch on the right needle.

3. Carry this stitch over your second knitted stitch on the right needle and over the tip of the right needle, and let it drop off the left needle. Knit another stitch and repeat steps 2 and 3.

4. Once you have cast off all your stitches, you will have a single stitch left on the right needle. Break the working yarn off the ball, slip the stitch off the needle and pass the end of the yarn through the last stitch and pull tightly.

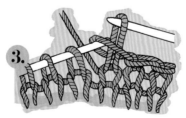

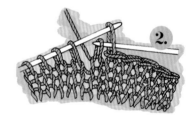

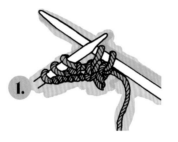

2. Basic stitches

How to knit

A knit stitch is the most basic type of stitch. Note that, when you knit a stitch, the working yarn stays at the back of the right needle.

1. With the working yarn at the back of the work, insert the right needle up through the bottom of the first stitch and to the back of the left needle, making a cross with the needles. Wrap the working yarn around the right needle, taking it behind the right needle and around it to bring it forwards between both needles.

2. Slide the right needle down through the top of the loop on the left needle and under towards the front of the left needle, pulling the yarn you wrapped around it through the loop. Pull the working yarn tight.

3. Slip the original stitch off the left needle.

4. Repeat steps 1–3 until all the stitches on the left needle have been knitted to complete the row.

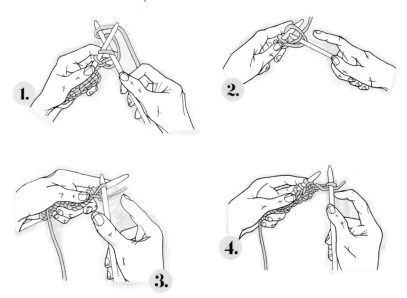

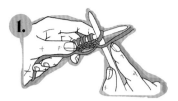

How to purl
A purl stitch is the second-most basic type of stitch and is the reverse of the knit stitch. Note that, when you purl a stitch, the working yarn stays at the front of the right needle.

1. With the working yarn at the front of the work, insert the right needle in through the top of the first stitch on the left needle and to the front, making a cross with the needles.

2. Take the working yarn back over and around the right needle and bring it under the needle to the front.

3. Slide the right needle down through the bottom of the loop on the left needle and back behind the left needle, pulling the yarn you wrapped around the right needle through the loop. Pull the working yarn tight.

4. Slip the original stitch off the left needle. Repeat steps 1–3 until all the stitches on the left needle have been purled to complete the row.

Basic stitch patterns

Once you know how to knit and purl, you can use these stitches to knit fabrics with various surface textures and patterns.

1. Garter stitch
Garter stitch is the most basic knitted fabric and is produced by simply knitting (or purling) each stitch on every single row. This forms a strong and firm pattern of raised horizontal ridges and the knitted fabric will not curl at the edges.

To knit in garter stitch, cast on any number of stitches and knit every stitch on every row. You can work garter stitch in purl stitch, with every stitch on every row being purled, but this is rarely done.

2. Stocking stitch

This is probably the most commonly used knitting stitch pattern. The side that is facing you when you knit a row is referred to as the right side (shown here), and the stitches are all purled when the wrong side is facing you. The pattern produced on the purl side is also known as reverse stocking stitch. This looks similar to garter stitch, but the ridges are slightly smaller and closer together in reverse stocking stitch.

To make stocking stitch, cast on any number of stitches. Knit 1 row of stitches, then purl the next. Repeat these 2 rows to the end.

3. Rib stitch

This fabric is composed of vertical 'ribs' of stitches. You can make a rib as wide or as narrow as you want by adjusting the number of stitches you knit and purl on each row.

To make double rib stitch (shown here), cast on a multiple of 4 stitches plus 2 extra. On the first row, knit 2, then purl 2, then knit 2 and repeat to the end. On the 2nd row, begin with 2 purl stitches, then 2 knit stitches and repeat to the end. Repeat these 2 rows to the end.

4. Moss stitch

This is one of my favourite stitches. It's not the quickest of stitches, as you need to keep lifting the yarn back and forth between stitches, but it produces a nice firm knitted fabric that doesn't curl at the edges. This fabric is usually created by casting on an odd number of stitches

To make moss stitch, cast on an odd number of stitches. On the first row, knit the first stitch, then pass the working yarn from the back of the work, between the needles to the front of the work, purl the next stitch, then pass the working yarn back between the needles to the back of the work, and repeat to the end of the row – you will finish on a knit stitch. Repeat on every row.

3. Shaping

To make a knitted fabric narrower, you reduce the number of stitches on the needle (known as decreasing). To make it wider, you increase the number of stitches on the needle (known as increasing). Use the following techniques to shape your knitted projects.

When stitches in a row are decreased using the technique 'knit 2 together' (K2tog), the stitch that has been eliminated from the row visibly slants to the right on a knit row, while 'purl 2 together' (p2tog) slants to the left on a purl row. The technique known as 'skpo' produces a decreased stitch that slants to the left on a knit row, and is often used at the opposite end of a row to 'k2tog' to produce mirror-image decreases at each end of the row.

Increasing
Making a stitch (M1)

1. Using your left needle, pick up the horizontal strand lying in between both needles.

2. Insert the right needle through the back of the picked-up strand on the left needle and knit it as usual.

Increasing a stitch (inc 1)

1. Insert the right needle into the first stitch on the left needle and knit it as usual, but do not slip the original stitch off the left needle.

2. Insert the right needle through the back of the same stitch on the left needle and knit the stitch again.

3. Slip the original stitch off the left needle. You now have 2 stitches on the right needle that have been knitted from 1 stitch.

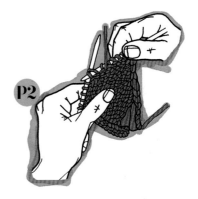

Decreasing

Knit 2 together (k2tog)

On a knit row, insert the right needle through the bottom of the next 2 stitches on your left needle and to the back, then knit them together.

Purl 2 together (p2tog)

On a purl row, insert the right needle through the top of the next 2 stitches on your left needle and to the front, then purl them together.

Slip 1, knit 1, pass slipped stitch over (skpo)

1. Insert the right needle through the bottom top of the next stitch on your left needle and slip it onto your right needle. Knit the next stitch.

2. Using your left needle, pick up the slipped stitch on your right needle and pass it over your knitted stitch and over the tip of the right needle, then let it drop off the left needle.

4. Sewing up

So you've got to the end of a pattern safely and you've cast off your project, but how do you put it together?

Take your time when sewing up: you put effort into knitting the project, so don't rush at this stage and spoil it.

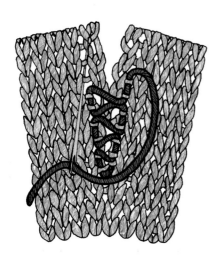

Mattress stitch
Using Mattress stitch is the best way of sewing knitted fabrics together as it creates a completely invisible seam, but it can take a little practice to get it right.

With the right sides of the knitting facing you, pick up the first 2 horizontal bars between the first and the second stitches on the left piece of knitting and pass the needle through. Now move across to the right piece and pick up the corresponding 2 bars on that piece.

Move back across to the left piece and pick up the 2 bars in between the next 2 stitches further up along the edge, then pick up the corresponding 2 bars on the opposite piece. Continue like this, firmly pulling the yarn to form the seam.

Rachel's tip:
Before you sew the pieces together you need to darn in any tails of yarn left from casting on and off, joining in new balls of yarn, or from colour work. Thread a darning needle with the tail and weave the needle through the backs of 4 or 5 adjacent stitches, pulling the yarn through them one by one. Then weave it back on itself to secure it. Do not pull the yarn too tight or the knitted fabric will pucker.

5. Colour work – Intarsia

The designs by Sarah Kim that appear in this book have all been knitted using the intarsia method. This technique is employed when creating blocks of different colours in a knitting project, and involves managing stitches of various colours on each row. Intarsia looks complicated, but it can be very simple. The following tips will make your project go more smoothly, and your end results better.

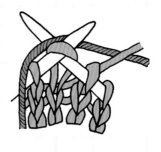

Always remember the phrase 'old over new' when it comes to using the intarsia technique and you can't go far wrong. Before you start to knit an intarsia design, the best thing to do is to wrap each coloured yarn about to be worked into the project around a bobbin. Each bobbin can hang at the back of the work. Using bobbins prevents the various yarns tangling.

On either the right (knit) or wrong (purl) side, when working the first stitch in a new yarn, insert the right needle into the stitch and pass the old working yarn over the new working yarn for the new shade. Knit or purl the following stitches in the new shade.

Use this technique each time you start working with a new shade of yarn. On the back of the knitted fabric the yarns will end up looped around each other along the colour joins, preventing unwanted holes appearing between colours on the right side of the fabric.

When you have finished the piece, weave in the tail ends at the back of the work. Steam the knitted project a little with an iron and a damp cloth – this will help to sort out any wonky stitches.

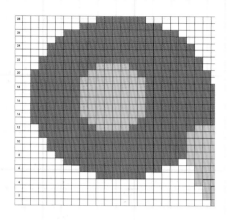

Following a chart/graph

When following a chart, you always start with a knit row and at the bottom right-hand side of the chart. The numbers on the chart indicate how many rows you should have done. So, you start at number 1 and read all the odd-numbered rows from right to left and the even-numbered rows from left to right. Each box on the chart represents 1 stitch and is usually coloured to match the yarn that should be used for that stitch.

6. *Using circular needles*

Knitting in the round is a technique that can be used when creating hats, scarfs, socks and sweaters. It enables you to produce a seamless piece of knitting and, therefore, no sewing up is required! It is important to ensure before you start that you have the right length of circular needle – using one that is too long will cause your stitches to stretch.

When knitting in the round, the right side of the work is always facing you, so there is no need to purl any stitches to achieve stocking stitch, unless you are working a decorative stitch. Firstly, cast on the required amount of stitches. Before joining the row into a round, ensure you check that all cast-on stitches are spaced evenly around the needle. With the start of the cast-on edge near the tip of the needle that's in your left hand, and the end of the cast on edge near the tip of the needle that's in your right hand, knit the first stitch on the left needle. The best thing to do at this point is to place a marker on your first stitch worked, which will enable you to keep track of where the beginning of a round is. Continue to knit all the stitches in the round, ensuring you continue to check for any twisted ones. Once you have knitted a few rows, knitting the stitches becomes easier and quicker.

7. Picking up stitches

Picking up stitches enables you to create really neat joins in your knitted project. It is used mainly when adding on earflaps, button holes, bands and edgings.

To pick up stitches along a cast-on or cast-off edge, working directly under the entire cast-on/-off stitch, insert the needle under the first stitch of the row, then carry the working yarn around the needle and draw a loop through the fabric to create a stitch on your needle. Repeat across the length of the cast-on/-off edge.

8. Abbreviations

alt	Alternate
approx	Approximately
DK	Double knitting
dec	Decrease
dpn(s)	Double-pointed needle(s)
inc	Increase
k	Knit
kfb	Knit into the front and back of the loop to create 2 stitches from 1
k2tog	Knit 2 stitches together
k2tbl	Knit 2 stitches together by inserting the right needle through the back of both stitches
M1	Make a stitch
p	Purl
psso	Pass slipped stitch over
p2tog	Purl 2 stitches together
rep	Repeat
RS	Right side
sl 1	Slip 1 stitch
skpo	Slip 1 stitch, knit 1 stitch, pass slipped stitch over
st(s)	Stitch(es)
st st	Stocking stitch
tbl	Through the back of loop(s)
WS	Wrong side
YF	Yarn forward
YO	Yarn over
YRN	Yarn round needle

CROCHET

1. Holding a crochet hook

Hold the hook in your right hand. You'll need your left hand to hold your work and the yarn. It's worth getting this positioning right, as the way you hold the yarn controls the tension and keeps it even. Practise both of the following methods to see which works best for you.

1. 2-finger grip
Take the working strand of yarn (the one attached to the ball) loosely around the back of the index and middle fingers on your left hand. Grip the yarn firmly with your last 2 fingers against your hand.

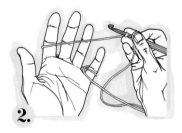

2. 1-finger grip
Take the working strand of the yarn around the back of the first 3 fingers on your left hand. Bring it in front of your little finger and wrap it right around that finger again. You can tighten your grip on the yarn by pressing your little finger against your ring finger.

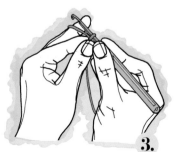

3. Holding the work
With the working strand of the yarn secure, take tight hold of your work with your left thumb and index finger close to the hook. Don't hold the hook too tight or your tension will be tight.

2. Basic techniques

To start any piece of crochet you need a foundation chain. It's just like a cast-on row in knitting and provides the basic foundation for the rest of the crocheted fabric. The number of chains you make determines the width of the fabric.

Slip knot

1. To start a foundation chain, leave a short tail of yarn and make a slip knot by winding the yarn twice around 2 fingers on your left hand. Hold the loose end of yarn secure with your thumb and take the second loop behind the first.

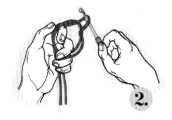

2. Pull the second loop of yarn through the first loop either with the crochet hook or your right-hand fingers.

3. Slip the new loop onto the crochet hook and tighten it up by gently pulling on the loose end of yarn. Remember not to make the slip knot too tight; you can slacken it off again by gently pulling on the working end of the yarn.

Making a foundation chain

1. Firmly hold the slip knot with your left index finger and thumb. Hold the crochet hook in your right hand. Lifting your left middle finger to tension the yarn, slide the hook over the working yarn from above (this often called 'yarn over' or 'yo'). Rotating the hook slightly, secure the yarn under the hook end.

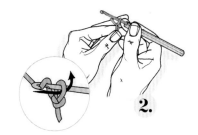

2. Pull the hook back through the slip knot. Repeat this process, continually adjusting your left-hand grip to hold the work near the hook, until the required number of chain stitches have been made.

Counting chain stitches

Count your chains before you begin the next row, then you'll be sure to make the right width of fabric. Make sure the foundation chain is not twisted and that the fronts of the chains are facing you. Count the number of loops – each one counts as 1 chain stitch. When you count, always ignore the initial slip knot and the loop on your hook.

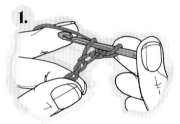

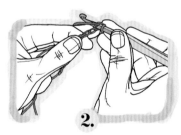

With the right length of foundation chain, you are ready to work the first row. This can be quite tricky if the foundation chain is tight and it can be hard to see each chain stitch. Here are 2 ways of working – either will make it easier.

Method 1
Flip the foundation chain over and slide the crochet hook from front to back through the top of the second chain stitch from the hook. Take the working yarn over the hook. Draw the yarn through the foundation chain stitch to make another loop on the hook. Complete the new chain stitch according to the pattern. Make the next stitch into the very next chain on the foundation chain. Continue in this way to the end.

Method 2
If you hold the foundation chain with the fronts of the chain stitches facing you, you can see that they each make a sideways 'v' shape. Slide the crochet hook from front to back under the second 'v' shape from the hook, ensuring it goes under 2 loops. Take the working yarn over the hook and draw it through so there's a loop on the hook. Complete the new stitch according to the pattern. Make the next stitch into the very next 'v' shape on the foundation chain. Continue in this way to the end.

Making a turning chain
To keep the shape of your crochet even, you need to make 1 or more turning chains at the beginning of each row. These are simple chain stitches and the number you need depends on the type of stitch in the next row. The number of stitches you need in your turning chain to match various stitches are given are as follows:

Double crochet: 1 turning chain.
Half treble crochet: 2 turning chains.
Treble crochet: 3 turning chains.
Double treble crochet: 4 turning chains.
When you work most stitches, count the turning chain as the first stitch. However, when you are working double crochet, ignore the turning chain – it doesn't count as a stitch.

3. Basic stitches

Here are a few stitches you can work into the foundation chain. They are all worked in the same basic way, but the differences are achieved by changing the number of times you wind the yarn around the hook and the number of loops you pull the hook through.

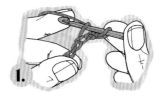

Slip stitch (ss)
This is used to sew up crocheted fabrics and to complete a round.

1. Slide the hook through the last chain stitch worked on the foundation chain, to produce 2 loops on the hook. Take the working yarn over the hook.

2. Draw the hook and yarn, back through both loops on the hook. Slide the hook through the next chain stitch on the foundation chain and repeat the process to the end of the row.

Working in rows
Always work from right to left along the rows. When you come to the end of a row you will need to turn your work. It doesn't matter whether you turn it clockwise or anti-clockwise – as long as you turn it the same way every time, the fabric will stay flat.

Your yarn should always be sitting at the back of your work before you make your chain stitches at the beginning of a new row. This will enable you to maintain a straight and neat edge.

1. Double crochet (dc)

This is one of the simplest and most commonly used crochet stitches.

1. At the beginning of the row, first add 1 extra chain stitch to make the turning chain. Then slide the hook into the second chain stitch on the foundation chain.

2. Take the working yarn over the hook and pull the yarn back through the first loop on the hook. Take the yarn over again and pull it back through both loops to produce just 1 new loop on the hook. Repeat steps 1–2 to the end of the row, working into the next chain stitch on the foundation chain.

3. At the end of the row, turn your work and make 1 turning chain. On all rows after the first, make double crochets in the same way as in steps 1 and 2, but sliding the hook under both loops at the top of each stitch (the 'v' shape described on page 28).

2. Treble crochet (tr)

Treble crochet produces an open fabric, because the yarn is wound around the hook 3 times to create long stitches.

1. At the beginning of the row, first add a turning chain of 3 extra stitches. Take the working yarn over the hook. Then slide the hook into the fourth chain from the hook on the foundation chain.

2. Take the yarn over the hook and pull it back through the first loop on the hook. You should now have 3 loops on the hook again.

3. Take the yarn over the hook and pull it back through the first 2 loops on the hook. You will now have 2 loops on the hook.

4. Take the yarn over the hook again and pull it back through the last 2 loops to give 1 new loop on the hook. Repeat steps 1–4 to the end of the row, working into each chain stitch on the foundation chain.

5. At the end of the row, turn your work and make 3 turning chains. On all rows after the first, make treble crochets into the trebles on the previous row in the same way as in steps 1–4, but missing the first treble and sliding the hook under both loops at the top of each stitch (the 'v' shape described on page 28). At the end of the row, work the last treble into the top of the turning chain.

3. Half treble (htr)

The name of this stitch describes it well – it's a slightly shorter version of the treble.

1. At the beginning of the row, first add a turning chain of 2 extra chain stitches. Take the working yarn over the hook. Then slide the hook into the third chain stitch on the foundation chain. Pull the yarn back through the first loop on the hook. You should now have 2 loops on your hook.

2. Take the yarn over the hook again and pull the yarn through both loops to give 1 new loop on the hook. Repeat steps 1–2 to the end of the row, working into each next chain stitch on the foundation chain.

3. At the end of the row, turn your work and make 2 turning chains. On all rows after the first, make half treble crochets into the half trebles on the previous row in the same way as in steps 1–2, but missing the first half treble and sliding the hook under both loops at the top of each stitch (the 'v' shaped described on page 28). At the end of the row, work the last half treble into the top of the turning chain.

4. Double treble (dtr)

This is a slightly taller stitch than the treble and gives you a very open fabric.

1. At the beginning of the row, first add a turning chain of 4 extra stitches. Take the working yarn over the hook twice. Then slide the hook into the fifth chain from the hook on the foundation chain. Take the yarn over the hook again, just once.

2. Pull the crochet hook through the first loop on the hook. You will now have 4 loops on the hook.

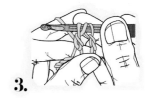

3. Now take the yarn over the hook again and pull it back through the first 2 loops on the hook. You will now have 3 loops left on the hook.

4. Repeat step 3, pulling the yarn through the next 2 loops on the hook. Repeat again and pull the yarn through the last 2 loops to give 1 remaining loop. Repeat steps 1–4 to the end of the row, working into each next chain stitch on the foundation row.

5. At the end of the row, turn your work and make 4 turning chains. On all rows after the first, make double treble crochets into the double trebles on the previous row in the same way as in steps 1–4, but missing the first double treble and sliding the hook under both loops at the top of each stitch (the 'v' shape described on page 28). At the end of the row, work the last double treble into the top of the turning chain.

4. The next step

Joining a new yarn

Always ensure you have enough yarn to crochet to the end of the row. But don't panic – if you run out, there's a way of joining new working yarn into your fabric.

1. Start to work in the end of the new yarn a few stitches before you finish the old yarn. Do this by laying it along the top of the previous row so that you work over it as you make the next few stitches.

2. When you need to change yarns, draw the first loops for the next stitch through with the old yarn. Then pick up the new yarn and draw it through to make the last loop of the stitch. Continue with the new yarn, working over the end of the old yarn to secure it. Neatly snip off the 2 ends of yarn.

Fastening off

When you've finished your crocheted fabric, you will need to fasten off.

Make 1 chain. Cut the yarn with a tail that's approximately 15cm/6in long. Then pull the tail firmly through the chain to secure it. Either leave the tail for sewing up later or weave it in.

Weaving in ends

Ends of yarn need to be woven carefully into the crocheted fabric so that they can't be seen and won't unravel. It's often convenient to weave them into a seam or, failing that, through the backs of stitches on the wrong side.

Thread the end into a tapestry needle, then weave it through the backs of several crochet stitches one by one. Don't pull the yarn tight or it will pucker the fabric. Carefully trim off the end.

5. *Shaping*

Shaping crocheted fabric is really simple. There are a few different methods to try, but each one will provide you with a nice neat increase or decrease.

Increasing a stitch

You may need to increase the number of stitches in order to widen the fabric at either or both ends of a row, to give it shape along a row or to keep the rounds in a circular shape flat. There is one basic method of doing this and it can be worked using any type of stitch.

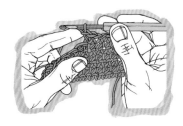

Simply work 2 or more stitches, depending on the pattern or the increase required, into 1 stitch on the previous row or round.

Decreasing a stitch

There are 2 ways of decreasing stitches – both can be worked using any type of stitch. Different patterns may suggest one or the other method, and each produces slightly different results.

The simplest way to decrease a stitch is to miss out working into the next stitch on the previous row or round, working into the one after it instead. Depending on the pattern or how many stitches you need to decrease, you can miss out 1 or more stitches along a row.

Alternatively, you can decrease a stitch by working 2 stitches together. For example with double crochet, draw the yarn through the next stitch on the previous row or round, but don't complete the stitch. You should now have 2 loops on your hook. Insert the hook into the next stitch on the previous row or round and draw the yarn through to produce 3 loops on the hook.

Take the yarn over the hook again and pull it through all 3 loops.

You can use this method to decrease more than 1 stitch by working into more stitches on the previous row or round and pulling the yarn through all the extra loops on the hook in one action.

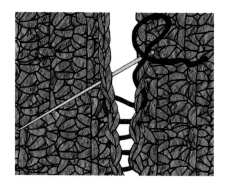

6. Sewing up

Woven seam
This invisible seam provides a neat flat finish that is suitable for garments and fine fabrics.

Place the 2 pieces of crocheted fabric side by side, aligning the stitches and with the right sides facing down. Thread a tapestry needle with matching yarn. Insert the needle from right to left through the loops of the first stitch on the right-hand fabric, then through the loops of the first stitch on the left-hand fabric. Now insert the needle from left to right through the loops of the second stitch on the left-hand, and then the right-hand fabric. Gently pull the yarn through and the crocheted pieces together.

Continue to work up the seam, 1 pair of stitches at a time, in the same way. After every few stitches, gently pull the yarn and draw the pieces together. Don't pull the yarn up too tightly because the seam should stretch as much as the crocheted fabric. Sew the ends of yarn into the seam and trim neatly.

Slip stitch seam
This method produces a firm seam, which is ideal for items such as bags that do not need to stretch much. You can work the seam on the wrong side, or on the right side to make a neat ridge.

Hold the 2 pieces of crocheted fabric together, aligning the stitches. Insert the crochet hook under both loops at the top of a pair of corresponding edge stitches. Draw through the yarn with the hook to make a slip stitch. Continue in the same way to complete the seam. Fasten off and trim the yarn ends.

7. Abbreviations

bdc:	Beaded double crochet	**MB:**	Make a bobble stitch
ch:	Chain	**rep:**	Repeat
ch sp:	Chain space	**RS:**	Right side
dc:	Double crochet	**ss:**	Slip stitch
dec:	Decrease	**sts:**	Stitches
dtr:	Double treble	**tr:**	Treble or triple crochet
hdc:	Half double treble	**tog:**	Together
htr:	Half treble crochet	**WS:**	Wrong side
inc:	Increase	**[ ]**	Repeat

FUN DECORATIONS

1. Embroidery stitches

1. Back stitch
Back stitches are a continuous row of stitches that join each other. Take your needle through from the back to the front of the fabric, leaving a small gap. Position your needle at the end of the last stitch worked and pass the needle to the back, then back through to the front again leaving a small gap. Repeat as necessary.

2. Satin stitch
These are used to completely cover a small section of a piece of fabric, which is easier to achieve if you mark out the shape you wish to embroider using some dressmaker's chalk, so you have a form to follow. Start at the bottom of the shape and work upwards, working lots of stitches close to one another, making them wider or narrower as necessary. You might also like to edge your satin-stitch design with a chain or back stitch.

3. Chain stitch
Chain stitches look like little flower petals. Pass the needle from the back to the front of the fabric, making sure you have a long tail of yarn for creating a few chain stitches. Make a small petal-shaped loop and position your needle so that it sits about 1cm down from the tip of the loop you have created (where you came through the fabric). Holding the loop with your left thumb, pass your needle from the front to the back of the fabric, then back through to the front, positioning your needle so that it passes through just before the tip of the loop you have created. Pull tightly to complete the chain stitch and repeat as necessary.

4. Blanket stitch
A blanket stitch is usually used to add a decorative edging to a piece of fabric. Pass your needle from the back to the front of the fabric, working a few millimeters in from the edge. Carry the needle downwards and take it under and through the loop created with the working yarn. Repeat as necessary.

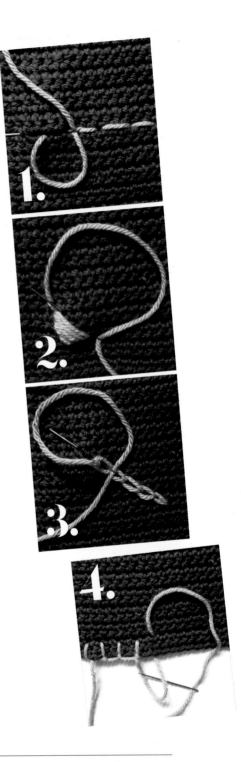

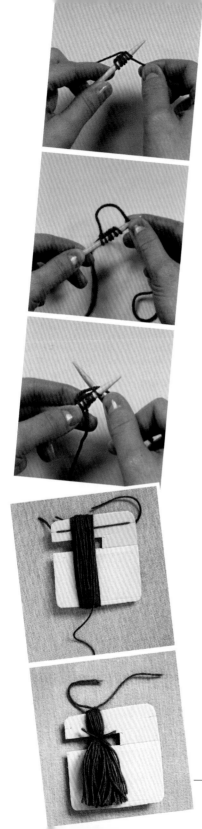

2. I-cords

Remember making knitted cords at primary school using a knitting dolly? The I-cord technique provides the same effect and it's very simple to create I-cord. All you need is 2 double pointed needles and some yarn.

Cast on the required number of stitches onto 1 of your dpns and knit all stitches.

Now slide all of your stitches worked to the other end of the dpn in your right hand and transfer that needle to your left hand.

With the working yarn at the back of the work, insert your right needle into the first stitch on the left needle. Pull the working yarn tightly up to the tip of the right needle and knit that stitch. Continue to knit the rest of the stitches along the row. Repeat in this way until you have the required length of fabric.

3. Tassels

Tassels are a nice alternative to pom poms. You would normally find these on the ends of curtain tie backs, wall hangings and scarves, but they also look great on hats!

Cut out a rectangular piece of strong card and make a slot at 1 side as shown in the picture opposite. Place a length of yarn around the top of the cardboard and tie it securely.

Wrap lots of yarn around from top to bottom of the rectangle – the amount of windings will depend on how chunky you want your tassel to be.

Now place a length of yarn around the tassel at the top of the slot and tie it securely with a double knot. Cut the yarn wrapped around the top of the cardboard at both ends and tie around the tassel securely with a double knot. Cut through all bottom loops to complete the tassel.

4. Pom poms

I love making pom poms and I make them in many different sizes and yarns, even combining different yarns in 1 pom pom. Nowadays, you can buy pom-pom makers, but I still prefer to make them the traditional way I was taught as a child.

1. Cut 2 circles of card of the same diameter and cut a small round hole in the middle of each circle. Align the card pieces, then tie the end of a long length of yarn around the pairing and knot it to secure. Wind your yarn through the holes in the middle of the 2 pieces of card and around the outer circles. Here's a tip – double up your yarn and it will take less time!!

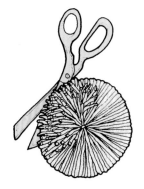

2. Repeat until you have the required amount of yarn wound around both circles. Then, using a pair of scissors, cut the yarn around the circumference of the circle, between both circles of card, so that the loops are cut open.

3. Separate the 2 circles of card slightly and tie a piece of strong embroidery thread tightly around the yarn visible through the gap between the cards. Then remove the cards. Use the embroidery thread to attach the pompom.

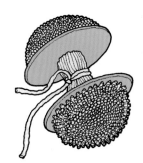

2

Adults

KNITTED POLAR BEAR HAT WITH EAR FLAPS

Rachel Henderson

If you like knitting in the round, this sweet polar bear hat is the perfect project for you, and it's ideal for when conditions are arctic.

Size: Adult (one size)

Materials needed:
~ Yarn A: 1 x 50g ball of Rowan Cocoon shade 801, Polar.
~ Yarn B: 1 x 50g ball of Rowan Cocoon shade 802, Alpine.
~ Oddment of black yarn.
~ Round marker.
~ Stuffing or toy filling.

Needles:
~ 1 set of 5mm (US 8) double-pointed needles.
~ 5mm (US 8) 40cm/15½in circular needle.
~ 4.5mm (US 7) crochet hook.

Tension:
19 sts and 25 rows to 10cm/4in square over st st using 5mm (US 8) needles.

Pattern:
Earflaps (make 2):
Using 2 x 5mm (US 8) dpns and yarn A, cast on 5 sts.
Row 1: k1, kfb, k1, kfb, k1 (7 sts).
Row 2: and every alt row: p to end.
Row 3: k1, kfb, k3, kfb, k1 (9 sts).
Row 5: k1, kfb, k5, kfb, k1 (11 sts).
Row 7: k1, kfb, k7, kfb, k1 (13 sts).
Row 9: k1, kfb, k9, kfb, k1 (15 sts).
Row 11: k1, kfb, k11, kfb, k1 (17 sts).
Row 13: k1, kfb, k13, kfb, k1 (19 sts).
Row 14: p to end.
Continue straight in st st until earflap measures 9cm/3½in.
Leave sts on spare needle.

Hat:
Using 5mm (US 8) circular needle and yarn A, cast on 8 sts.
With RS facing, knit across 19 sts of first earflap, cast on 23 sts, k across 19 sts of second earflap, then cast on 8 sts (77 sts).
Join into a circle and place round marker. Work in the round in st st (k every round) until hat measures 14cm/5½in from cast on edge. Begin shaping. (Change to dpns when necessary.)
Round 1: *k5, k2tog, rep from * to end (66 sts).
Round 2: and every alt round: k to end.
Round 3: *k4, k2tog, rep from * to end (55 sts).
Round 5: *k3, k2tog, rep from * to end (44 sts).
Round 7: *k2, k2tog, rep from * to end (33 sts).
Round 9: *k1, k2tog, rep from * to end (22 sts).
Round 10: *k2tog, rep from * to end (11 sts).
Round 11: k2tog to last st, k1.
Break off yarn, thread it through the remaining sts and fasten off securely.

Knitted mouth:

Using 4 x 5mm (US 8) dpns and yarn A, cast on 24 sts (8 sts on each of 3 needles). Join into a circle and place round marker.
K 4 rounds.
Round 5: *k2tog, repeat from * to end of round (12 sts).
Round 6–7: k to end.
Round 8: *k3tog, repeat from * to end of round (4 sts).
Break off yarn, thread it through the remaining sts and fasten off securely.

Ears (make 2):

Using 4 x 5mm (US 8) dpns and yarn A, cast on 30 sts (10 sts on each of 3 needles). Join into circle and place round marker.
K 6 rounds.
Round 7: *k2tog, repeat from * to end (15 sts).
Rounds 8–10: k to end.
Round 11: *k2tog, repeat from * to last st, k1 (8 sts).
Round 12: k to end.
Round 13: *k2tog, repeat from * to end (4 sts).
Break off yarn, thread it through the remaining sts and fasten off securely.

Making up:

Weave in all ends. Using 4.5mm (US 7) crochet hook and yarn B, work 2 rows of double crochet (see page 30) around the edge of the hat and earflaps. Position the ears on the sides of the hat 5cm/2in from the centre-top, using the picture opposite to guide you, and attach them to the hat using an overstitch. Stuff the muzzle with toy filling. Position it on the front of the hat using the picture opposite to guide you, and attach it using an overstitch.

Embroider the nose and mouth using satin stitch and backstitch (see page 37). Embroider the eyes using satin stitch (see page 37).

Make 2 I-cords (see page 38), each 25cm/10in in length, using yarn A. Attach a cord to each earflap.

Using yarn B, make 2 pom poms (see page 39), each with an 8cm/3¼in diameter. Attach 1 pom pom to the end of each cord.

OWL TEABAG HAT

Sarah Kim

Know any wise owls that would look cool in this hat?
The owl face motif is fun to knit on this simple, trendy teabag-style hat.

Size: Adult (one size)

Materials:
~ Yarn A: 1 x 50g ball of Rowan Felted Tweed DK shade 153, Phantom.
~ Yarn B: 1 x 50g ball of Rowan Felted Tweed DK shade 177, Clay.
~ Yarn C: 1 x 50g ball of Rowan Felted Tweed DK shade 160, Gilt.
~ 2 x brown buttons.

Needles:
~ 1 pair of 3.25mm (US 3) needles.
~ 1 pair of 4mm (US 6) needles.

Tension:
22 sts and 30 rows to 10cm/4in square over st st using 4mm (US 6) needles.

Pattern:
Using 3.25mm (US 3) needles and yarn A, cast on 127 sts.
Row 1: k1, *p1, k1, rep from * to end.
Row 2: p1, *k1, p1, rep from * to end.
These 2 rows set the 1 x 1 rib. Cont in rib for 6 more rows, ending with RS facing for next row.
Change to 4mm (US 6) needles.
Row 1: k63 in yarn A, join yarn C, k1, change back to yarn A, k63. This completes row 1 of the chart, shown on page 49, with the single yarn-C stitch marking the central stitch on the chart (and the centre-front of the hat).
Starting with a p row, working in st st, using the intarsia technique (see page 23) and yarns A, B and C, continue to follow the chart until all 28 rows have been completed. (Note that odd numbered rows should be knitted and even numbered rows should be purled.) End with RS facing for next row. Break off yarns B and C. Using yarn A, continue straight in st st until work measures 21cm/8½in.
Cast off.

Making up:
Weave in all ends. Sew together the side edges of the hat using mattress stitch (see page 22). This seam marks the centre-back of the hat.
Ensuring the seam is centred, sew along the cast off edge at the top of the hat using mattress stitch.
Sew a button in the centre of each yarn-C circle to form the eyes.

Chart

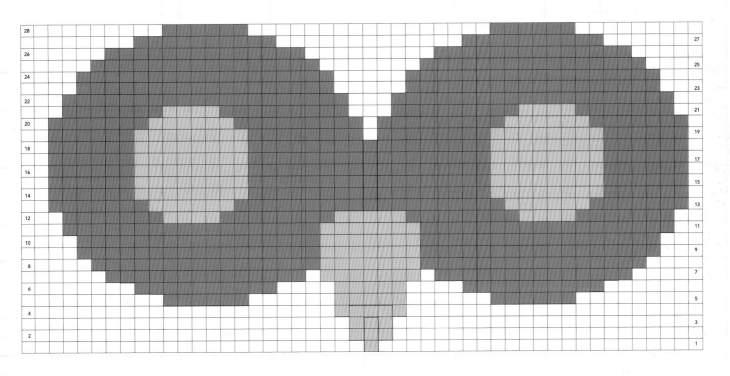

Yarn A   Yarn B   Yarn C

FOX BEANIE HAT

Sarah Kim

You don't have to be quick as a fox at knitting to run up this beanie speedily. As it's quick and easy to make, it's a great project for beginners who are new to the intarsia technique.

Size: Adult (one size)

Materials:
~ Yarn A: 2 x 50g balls Rowan Lima shade 885, Machu Picchu.
~ Yarn B: 1 x 50g ball Rowan Lima shade 890, Bolivia.
~ Yarn C: 1 x 50g ball Rowan Lima shade 893, Argentina.
~ 2 x black buttons.

Needles:
~ 1 pair of 4.5mm (US 7) needles.
~ 1 pair of 5.5mm (US 9) needles.

Tension:
20 sts and 26 rows to 10cm/4in square over stocking stitch using 5.5mm (US 9) needles.

Pattern:
Using 4.5mm (US 7) needles and yarn A, cast on 30 sts. Join yarn B and cast on 38 sts, then change back to yarn A and cast on 30 sts (98 sts). The central 38 yarn-B sts, and 1 yarn-A st on either side of those, are to be worked following the chart, shown on page 53.

Using the intarsia technique (see page 23), follow the chart using yarns A and B, and working as follows:
Row 1: *k1, p1, rep from * to end.
Row 2: *k1, p1, rep from * to end.
These 2 rows set the 1 x 1 rib.

Continuing to follow the chart, work 4 more rows in 1 x 1 rib, ending with RS facing for next row.

Change to 5.5mm (US 9) needles.

Starting with a k row (Row 7 on the chart), work in st st using yarns A, B and C until all 16 rows of the chart have been completed. (Note that odd-numbered rows should be knitted and even numbered rows should be purled.)

Break off yarns B and C and, using yarn A, continue in st st until work measures 15cm/6in, ending with RS facing for next row. Begin shaping:
Row 1: k7, k2tog, *k6, k2tog, rep from * to last st, k1 (86 sts).
Rows 2–4: Work in st st, starting with a p row.
Row 5: k6, k2tog, *k5, k2tog, rep from * to last st, k1 (74 sts).
Rows 6–8: Work in st st, starting with a p row.
Row 9: k5, k2tog, *k4, k2tog, rep from * to last st, k1 (62 sts).

Row 10 and every alt row: p to end.
Row 11: k4, k2tog, *k3, k2tog, rep from * to last st, k1 (50 sts).
Row 13: k3, k2tog, *k2, k2tog, rep from * to last st, k1 (38 sts).
Row 15: k2, k2tog, *k1, k2tog, rep from * to last st, k1 (26 sts).
Row 17: k1, k2tog to last st, k1 (14 sts).
Break off yarn, thread it through the remaining st and fasten off securely.

Ears:

Outer ears (make 2):
Using 5.5mm (US 9) needles and yarn A, cast on 15 sts.
Starting with a k row (RS), work 12 rows in st st.
Change to yarn C.
Row 13: k1, s1, k1, psso, k9, k2tog, k1 (13 sts).
Row 14 and every alt row: p to end.
Row 15: k1, s1, k1, psso, k7, k2tog, k1 (11 sts).
Row 17: k1, s1, k1, psso, k5, k2tog, k1 (9 sts).
Row 19: k1, s1, k1, psso, k3, k2tog, k1 (7 sts).
Row 21: k1, s1, k1, psso, k1, k2tog, k1 (5 sts).
Row 23: k1, s1, k2tog, psso, k1 (3 sts).
Row 24: p3tog.
Break off yarn, thread it through the remaining st and fasten off securely.

Inner ears (make 2):
Using 5.5mm (US 9) needles and yarn B, cast on 13 sts.
Starting with a k row (RS), work 12 rows in st st.
Row 13: k1, s1, k1, psso, k7, k2tog, k1 (11 sts).
Row 14 and every alt row: p to end.
Row 15: k1, s1, k1, psso, k5, k2tog, k1 (9 sts).
Row 17: k1, s1, k1, psso, k3, k2tog, k1 (7 sts).
Row 19: k1, s1, k1, psso, k1, k2tog, k1 (5 sts).
Row 21: k1, s1, k2tog, psso, k1 (3 sts).
Row 22: p3tog.
Break off yarn, thread it through the remaining st and fasten off securely.

Making up:
Weave in all ends.
Sew the side edges of the hat using mattress stitch (see page 22). The seam marks the centre-back of the hat.
Sew 1 inner-ear piece to 1 outer-ear piece (ensuring the RS of each piece faces outwards) using mattress stitch (see page 22). Repeat with the remaining ear pieces.
Position the ears to the hat using the pictures to guide you, then attatch them to the hat.
Position the buttons using the pictures to guide you, then sew on the buttons to form the eyes.

Chart

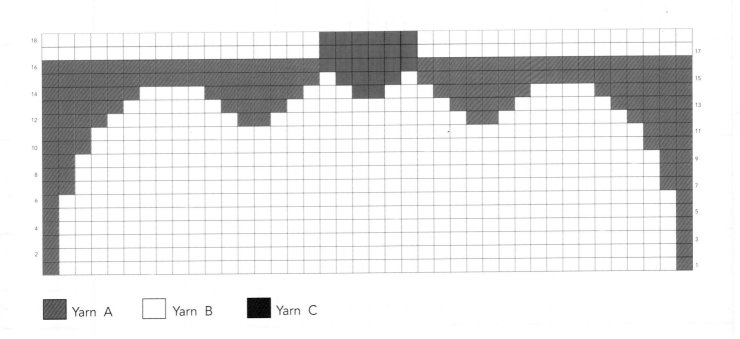

	Yarn A		Yarn B		Yarn C

KNITTED PENGUIN HAT

Rachel Henderson

Mr Penguin with his dapper bow tie is knitted using a wonderfully soft wool and alpaca blend. The ribbing gives this jolly hat a nice and snug fit.

Size: Adult (one size)

Materials needed:
~ Yarn A: 1 x 50g ball of Rowan Creative Focus Worsted shade 00500, Ebony.
~ Yarn B: 1 x 50g ball of Rowan Creative Focus Worsted shade 02055, Carmine.
~ Yarn C: 1 x 50g ball of Rowan Creative Focus Worsted shade 02190, Copper.
~ White felt.
~ White embroidery thread.
~ 2 x black buttons.

Needles:
~ 1 pair of 4.5mm (US 7) needles.

Tension:
20 sts and 24 rows to 10cm/4in square over st st.

Pattern:
Using yarn A, cast on 110 sts.
Next row: *k1, p1, repeat from * to end.
Repeat previous row until work measures 14cm/5½in.
Begin shaping.
Row 1: *(k1, p1) x 4, k2tog, rep from * to end (99 sts).
Row 2: *(p1, k1) x 4, p1, rep from * to end (99 sts).
Row 3: *(k1 p1) x 3, k1, p2tog, rep from * to end (88 sts).
Row 4: *k1, p1, rep from * to end (88 sts).
Row 5: *(k1, p1) x 3, k2tog, rep from * to end (77 sts).
Row 6 and every alt row: k the k sts and p the p sts.
Row 7: *(k1, p1) x 2, k1, p2tog, rep from * to end (66 sts).
Row 9: *(k1, p1) x 2, k2tog, rep from * to end (55 sts).
Row 11: *k1, p1, k1, p2tog, rep from * to end (44 sts).
Row 13: *k1, p1, k2tog, rep from * to end (33 sts).
Row 15: *k1, p2tog, rep from * to end (22 sts).
Row 16: *k3tog, rep from * to last st, k1 (8 sts).
Break off yarn, thread it through the remaining sts and fasten off securely.

Beak:
Using yarn C, cast on 3 sts.
Row 1: k1, kfb, k1 (4 sts).
Row 2 and every alt row: p to end.
Row 3: k1, kfb twice, k1 (6 sts).
Row 5: k1, kfb, k2, kfb, k1 (8 sts).
Row 7: k1, kfb, k4, kfb, k1 (10 sts).
Row 9: k1, kfb, k6, kfb, k1 (12 sts).
Row 11: k1, kfb, k8, kfb, k1 (14 sts).
Row 13: k1, kfb, k10, kfb, k1 (16 sts).
Cast off.

Bow:

Using yarn B, cast on 10 sts.

Next row: *k1, p1, repeat from * to end.

Repeat previous row until work measures 9cm/3½in.

Cast off.

Middle band:

Using yarn B, cast on 4 sts.

Next row: *k1, p1, repeat from * to end.

Repeat previous row until work measures 2.5cm/1in.

Cast off.

Wrap the middle band around the centre of the bow, stitching together the cast on and cast off edges of the band.

Eyes (make 2):

Trace the template shown left onto white card and cut it out. Pin the template onto the white felt, draw around it twice and cut out the circles.

Making up:

Weave in all ends.

Sew the edges of the hat together using mattress stitch (see page 22). The seam marks the centre-back of the hat.

Position the beak onto the front of the hat, using the picture opposite to guide you, and attach it to the hat using an overstitch.

Position the bow just under the bottom of the beak, using the picture opposite to guide you, and attach it to the hat.

Stitch a black button onto the centre of each white felt circle. Position these on the front of the hat, using the picture opposite to guide you, and sew them onto the hat.

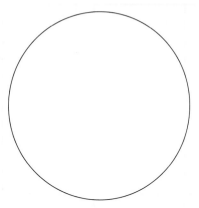

Template for eye

WOLF BEANIE HAT

Sarah Kim

Simple, yet effective, this lovely wolf-inspired hat is easy to make and knits up quickly - the ideal gift when you don't have much time.

Size: Adult (one size)

Materials:

~ Yarn A: 2 x 50g balls of Rowan Lima shade 893, Argentina.
~ Yarn B: 1 x 50g balls of Rowan Lima shade 890, Bolivia.
~ Yarn C: 1 x 50g balls of Rowan Lima shade 896, Ecuador.
~ 2 black buttons.
~ Oddments of black yarn.

Needles:

~ 1 pair of 4.5mm (US 7) needles.
~ 1 pair of 5.5mm (US 9) needles.

Tension:

20sts and 26 rows to 10cm/4in square over st st using 5.5mm (US 9) needles.

Pattern:

Hat:

Using 4.5mm (US 7) needles and yarn A, cast on 40 sts, join yarn B and cast on 19 sts, change back to yarn A and cast on 40 sts (99 sts). The central yarn-B sts, and the 5 yarn-A sts on either side of those, are to be worked following the chart, shown on page 61. Using the intarsia technique (see page 23), follow the chart using yarns A and B, working as follows:

Row 1: *k1, p1, rep from * to last st, k1.
Row 2: *p1, k1, rep from * to last st, p1.
These 2 rows set the 1 x 1 rib.
Continuing to follow the chart, work 4 more rows in 1 x 1 rib, ending with RS facing for next row.
Change to 5.5mm (US 9) needles. Starting with a k row (Row 7 on the chart), work in st st using yarns A and B until all 30 rows of chart have been completed. (Note that odd-numbered rows should be knitted and even numbered rows should be purled.)

Break off yarn B and, using yarn A, continue in st st until work measures 15cm/6in, ending with RS facing for next row.
Begin shaping.
Row 1: k2tog, *k6, k2tog, rep from * to last st, k1 (86 sts).
Rows 2–4: Work 3 rows in st st.
Row 5: k6, k2tog, *k5, k2tog, rep from * to last st, k1 (74 sts).
Rows 6–8: Work 3 rows in st st.
Row 9: k5, k2tog, *k4, k2tog, rep from * to last st, k1 (62 sts).
Row 10 and every alt row: p to end.
Row 11: k4, k2tog, *k3, k2tog, rep from * to last st, k1 (50 sts).
Row 13: k3, k2tog, *k2, k2tog, rep from * to last st, k1 (38 sts).
Row 15: k2, k2tog, *k1, k2tog, rep from * to last st, K1 (26 sts).
Row 17: k1, k2tog to last st, k1 (14 sts).

Break off yarn, thread it through the remaining sts and fasten off securely.

Ears:
Outer (make 2):
Using 5.5mm (US 9) needles and yarn A, cast on 13 sts. Starting with a knit row (RS), work 12 rows st st.
Row 13: k1, s1, k1, psso, k7, k2tog, k1 (11 sts).
Row 14 and every alt row: p to end.
Row 15: k1, s1, k1, psso, k5, k2tog, k1 (9 sts).
Row 17: k1, s1, k1, psso, k3, k2tog, k1 (7 sts).
Row 19: k1, s1, k1, psso, k1, k2tog, k1 (5 sts).
Row 21: k1, s1, k2tog, psso, k1 (3 sts).
Row 22: p3tog.
Break off yarn, thread it through the remaining st and fasten off securely.

Inner ears (make 2):
Using 5.5mm (US 9) needles and yarn C, cast on 11sts.
Starting with a k row (RS), work 12 rows st st.
Row 13: k1, s1, k1, psso, k5, k2tog, k1 (9 sts).
Row 14 and every alt row: p to end.
Row 15: k1, s1, k1, psso, k3, k2tog, k1 (7 sts).
Row 17: k1, s1, k1, psso, k1, k2tog, k1 (5 sts).
Row 19: k1, s1, k2tog, psso, k1 (3 sts).
Row 20: p3tog
Break off yarn, thread it through the remaining st and fasten off securely.

Making up:
Weave in all ends.
Sew the edges of the hat using mattress stitch (see page 22). The seam marks the centre-back of the hat.
Sew 1 inner-ear piece to 1 outer-ear piece, ensuring the RS of each piece face outwards. Repeat with the remaining ear pieces. Position the ears to the hat using the picture opposite to guide you, then attatch them to the hat.
Using black yarn, embroider the nose. The nose should be positioned just below the 3sts in yarn A in the centre of row 13 on the chart.

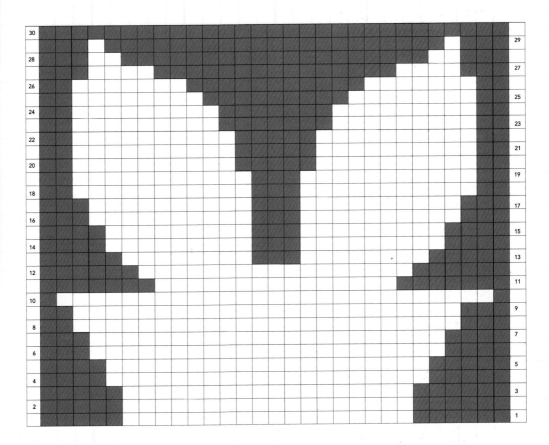

■ Yarn A   □ Yarn B

KNITTED DOG HAT

Rachel Henderson

Perfect for either guys or girls, this adorable doggy hat is made using a luxuriously soft yarn that contains baby alpaca and merino wool, so it is warm and extremely comfortable to wear.

Size: Adult (one size)

Materials needed:
~ Yarn A: 1 x 50g ball of Rowan Lima shade 890, Bolivia.
~ Yarn B: 1 x 50g ball of Rowan Lima shade 888, Lima.
~ White card, pencil and paper scissors.
~ Small piece of brown felt.
~ Fabric scissors.
~ 1 x brown button.
~ 1 x small black button.
~ Black yarn/embroidery thread.

Needles:
~ 1 pair of 5mm (US 8) needles.

Tension:
20 stitches and 26 rows to 10cm/4in square over st st.

Pattern:
Using yarn A, cast on 110 sts.
K 5 rows in garter stitch.
Break off yarn and attach yarn B. Continue in st st until work measures 14cm/5½in from cast on edge.
Begin shaping.
Row 1: *k8, k2tog, rep from * to end (99 sts).
Row 2 and every alt row: p to end.
Row 3: *k7, k2tog, rep from * to end (88 sts).
Row 5: *k6, k2tog, rep from * to end (77 sts).
Row 7: *k5, k2tog, rep from * to end (66 sts).
Row 9: *k4, k2tog, rep from * to end (55 sts).
Row 11: *k3, k2tog, rep from * to end (44 sts).
Row 13: *k2, k2tog, rep from * to end (33 sts).
Row 15: *k1, k2tog, rep from * to end (22 sts).
Row 16: *p3tog, rep from * to last st, p1 (88 sts).
Break off yarn, thread it through the remaining sts and fasten off securely.

Ears (make 2):
Using yarn A, cast on 40 sts.
Work 10cm/4in in st st, ending with a p row.
Next row: *k2tog, rep from * to end (20 sts).
Next 3 rows: Work in st st, starting with a p row.
Next row: *k2tog, rep from * to end (10 sts).
Next row: p to end.
Next row: *k3tog, rep from * to last st, k1 (4 sts).
Break off yarn, thread it through the remaining sts and fasten off securely.

Eye patch:

Trace the template shown below left onto card and cut it out. Pin the card template onto the brown felt, draw around it and cut it out.

Making up:

Sew the edges of the hat together using mattress stitch (see page 22).

Position the ears on the hat using the pictures to guide you, then attach them to the hat using a mattress stitch. Fold each ear over to create a floppy ear effect, and secure with a few stitches at the back of each.

Position the brown felt eye patch on the front of hat as shown in the picture left. Attach it using a large cross stitch and yarn A.

Position the brown button as the left eye, as shown in the picture, and attach it using yarn A.

Sew a small black button onto the hat for the nose using black embroidery thread.

Embroider the mouth, using the pictures to guide you, using backstitch (see page 37).

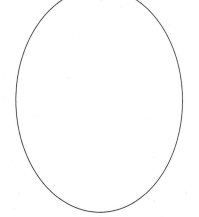

Template for eye patch

SOCK MONKEY EARFLAP HAT

Sarah Kim

Channel your inner monkey in this cheeky little hat! The earflaps make it extra warm, so you can monkey around outdoors to your heart's content!

Size: Adult (one size)

Materials:
~ Yarn A: 1 x 50g ball of Rowan Lima, shade 895, Brazil.
~ Yarn B: 1 x 50g ball of Rowan Lima, shade 890, Bolivia.
~ Yarn C: 1 x 50g ball of Rowan Lima, shade 891, La Paz.
~ Stitch holders.
~ 2 x small brown buttons.
~ 2 x medium-sized brown buttons.

Needles:
~ 1 pair of 5.5mm (US 9) needles.

Tension:
20 sts and 26 rows to 10cm/4in over st st.

Pattern:
Earflaps (make 2):
Using yarn A, cast on 4 sts.
Row 1: p to end.
Row 2 (RS): k2, YO, k2 (5 sts).
Row 3 and every alternate row: p to end.
Row 4: k1, m1, k3, m1, k1 (7 sts).
Row 6: k1, m1, k5, m1, k1 (9 sts).
Row 8: k1, m1, k7, m1, k1 (11 sts).
Row 10: k1, m1, k9, m1, k1 (13 sts).
Row 12: k1, m1, k11, m1, k1 (15 sts).
Row 14: k to end.
Row 16: k1, m1, k13, m1, k1 (17 sts).
Row 18: k to end.
Row 20: k1, m1, k15, m1, k1 (19 sts).
Row 22: k to end.
Row 24: k1, m1, k17, m1, k1 (21 sts).
Row 26: k to end.
Next row: p to end.
Break off yarn and leave the 21 sts on a stitch holder.

Hat:
Row 1: Using yarn A, cast on 11 sts, k across 21 sts of first earflap, cast on 5 sts, join yarn B and cast on 24 sts. Change back to yarn A and cast on 5 sts, k across 21 sts of second earflap, then cast on 11 sts (98 sts). This completes row 1 of the chart, shown on page 69. The central 24 sts are to be worked following the chart.

Starting with a p row (Row 2 on the chart), continue to follow the chart, working in st st and using the intarsia technique (see

page 23) until all 17 rows of the chart have been completed. (Note that odd-numbered rows should be knitted and even-numbered rows should be purled.) Break off yarn B.
Using yarn A, work 8 more rows in st st.

Break off yarn A and join yarn C. Work 3 rows in st st.

Break off yarn C and join yarn B. Continue in st-st until work measures 19cm/7½in from row 1, ending with RS facing for next row.

Next row: k3, k2tog, *(k2, k2tog), repeat from * to last st, k1 (74 sts).
Next row: p to end.
Next row: k2, k2tog, *(k1, k2tog), repeat from * to last st, k1 (50 sts).
Next row: p to end.
Next row: k1, *k2tog, repeat from * to last st, k1 (25 sts).
Break of yarn, thread it through the remaining sts and fasten off securely.

Ears (make 2):
Using yarn A, cast on 10 sts.
Work 8 rows in st st, starting with a k row.
Next row: k1, k1, sl1, psso, k4, k2tog, k1 (8 sts).
Next row: p1, p2tog, p2, p2tog tbl, p1 (6 sts).
Next row: k1, m1, k4, m1, k1 (8 sts).
Next row: p1, m1, k6, m1, p1 (10 sts).
Continue in st st for 8 more rows.
Cast off.

Pom poms:
Using yarn C, make 1 x 6cm/2¼in pom pom and 2 x 4cm/1½in pom poms (see page 39).

Making up:
Sew the edges of the hat together using mattress stitch (see page 22). The seam marks the centre-back of the hat.

Sew the side edges of the ears together using mattress stitch.

Position the ears on the hat just below the 3 rows knitted using yarn C, using the pictures to guide you, then attach them to the hat.

Position the buttons onto the hat using the picture opposite to guide you – the larger buttons are for the eyes, and the smaller ones are for the nose. Sew them onto the hat.

Sew the large pom pom to the top of the hat.

Plaited tassels:
Cut 12 x 90cm/35in strands yarn C.
Align 6 of these and fold them in half. Thread the middle of the strands through the gap made by the YO in row 2 of one earflap to form a loop. Draw the ends through the loop and pull tight to create a length of 12 strands. Create 3 groups of 4 strands and plait these tightly. Secure the end. Sew 1 4cm/1½in pom pom to the end of the tassel.

Repeat with the other 6 tassel strands and earflap.

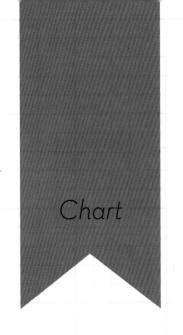

Chart

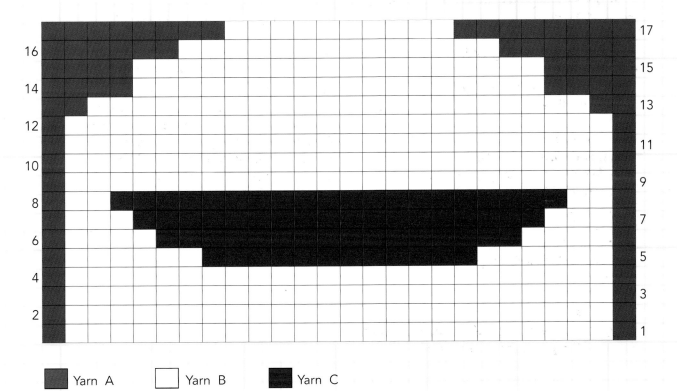

Yarn A   Yarn B   Yarn C

COW EARFLAP HAT

Sarah Kim

An "udderly" cute cow hat, complete with ear flaps and pom pom tassels.

Size: Adult (one size).

Materials:
~ Yarn A: 1 x 50g ball of Rowan Pure Wool DK shade 013, Enamel.
~ Yarn B: 1 x 50g ball of Rowan Pure Wool DK shade 004, Black.
~ Yarn C: 1 x 50g ball of Rowan Pure Wool DK shade 025, Tea Rose.
~ Yarn D: 1 x 50g ball of Rowan Pure Wool 4 ply shade 454, Gerbera.
~ 2 x black buttons.
~ Stuffing or toy filler.
~ Stitch holder.

Needles:
~ 1 pair of 4mm (US 6) needles.

Tension:
22 sts and 30 rows to 10cm/4in square over st st.

Pattern:
Right ear flap:
Using yarn A, cast on 4 sts.
P to end.
Row 1 (RS): k2, yo, k2 (5 sts).
Row 2: p1, m1, p3, m1, p1 (7 sts).
Row 3: k1, m1, k5, m1, k1 (9 sts).

Row 4: p1, m1, p7, m1, p1 (11 sts).
Row 5: k1, m1, k8, m1, k1 (13 sts).
Row 6: p1, m1, p11, m1, p1 (15 sts).
Row 7: k1, m1, k13, m1, k1 (17 sts).
Row 8: p1, m1, p15, m1, p1 (19 sts).
Row 9: k1, m1, k17, m1, k1 (21 sts).
Row 10: p1, m1, p19, m1, p1 (23 sts).
Row 11: k to end.
Row 12: p1, m1, p21, m1, p1 (25 sts).
Row 13: k to end.
Row 14: p1, m1, p23, m1, p1 (27 sts).
Rows 15–22: Work in st st, starting with k row.
Row 23: k1, m1, k25, m1, k1 (29 sts).
Row 24: p1, m1, p27, m1, p1 (31 sts).
Break off yarn and leave the remaining 31 sts on a stitch holder.

Left ear flap:
Using yarn A, cast on 4 sts. P to end. Work shaping as for right ear flap, but follow chart on page 73 for colour patterning. Row 1 of shaping corresponds to row 1 of the chart.

Hat:
Using yarn A, cast on 9 sts, then k across 4 sts of left ear flap. Join yarn B and k the remaining 27 sts of the left ear flap, then cast on 3 sts. Change back to yarn A and cast on 8 sts. Join yarn C and cast on 22 sts. Change back to yarn A and cast on 11 sts, k across 31 sts of right ear flap, cast on 9 sts (124 sts). This completes Row 1 of the chart, shown on page 73.

Starting with a p row, working in st st, using the intarsia technique (see page 23), continue to follow the chart until Row 42 of the chart has been completed. (Note that odd-numbered rows should be knitted and even-numbered rows should be purled.)

Begin shaping.

Row 43: k1, k2tog, *k8, k2tog, rep from * to last st, k1 (111 sts).

Rows 44–46: Work in st st, starting with a p row.

Row 47: k2, *k7, k2tog, rep from * to last st, k1 (99 sts).

Row 48: p to end.

Row 49: k2, *k6, k2tog, rep from * to last st, k1 (87 sts).

Row 50: p to end.

Row 51: k2, *k5, k2tog, rep from * to last st, k1 (75 sts).

Row 52: p to end.

Row 53: k2, *k4, k2tog, rep from * to last st, k1 (63 sts).

Row 54: p1, *p2tog, p3, rep from * to last 2sts, p2 (51 sts).

Row 55: k2, *k2, k2tog, rep from * to last st, k1 (39 sts).

Row 56: p1, *p2tog, p1, rep from * to last 2sts, p2 (27 sts).

Row 57: k2, *k2tog, rep from * to last st, k1 (15 sts).

Break off yarn, thread it through the remaining 15 sts and fasten off securely.

Outer ears (make 2):

Using yarn A, cast on 13 sts.

Starting with a k row (RS), work 12 rows st st.

Row 13: k1, s1, k1, psso, k7, k2tog, k1 (11 sts).

Row 14 and every alt row: p to end.

Row 15: k1, s1, k1, psso, k5, k2tog, k1 (9 sts).

Row 17: k1, s1, k1, psso, k3, k2tog, k1 (7 sts).

Row 19: k1, s1, k1, psso, k1, k2tog, k1 (5 sts).

Row 21: k1, s1, k2tog, psso, k1 (3 sts).

Row 22: p3tog.

Break off yarn, thread it through the remaining st and fasten off securely.

Inner ears (make 2):

Using yarn C, cast on 11 sts.

Starting with a k row (RS), work 12 rows st st.

Row 13: k1, s1, k1, psso, k5, k2tog, k1 (9 sts).

Row 14 and every alt row: p to end.

Row 15: k1, s1, k1, psso, k3, k2tog, k1 (7 sts).

Row 17: k1, s1, k1, psso, k1, k2tog, k1 (5 sts).

Row 19: k1, s1, k2tog, psso, k1 (3 sts).

Row 20: p3tog.

Break off yarn, thread it through the remaining st and fasten off securely.

Horns (make 2):

Using 2 strands of yarn D, cast on 16 sts.

Starting with a k row, work 8 rows in st st.

Row 9: *k1, k2tog, k1, rep from * to end (12 sts).

Rows 10–12: Work in st st, starting with a p row.

Row 13: *k2tog, rep from * to end (6 sts).

Row 14: p to end.

Row 15: *k2tog, rep from * to end (3 sts).

Row 16: p3tog.

Break off yarn, thread it through the remaining st and fasten off securely.

Pom poms:

Using yarn C, make 2 pom poms (see page 39), each with a 4cm/1½in diameter.

Making up:

Weave in all ends. Sew the side edges of the hat using mattress stitch (see page 22). The seam marks the centre-back of the hat. Position the buttons using the pictures to guide you, then sew them on to form eyes. Sew 1 inner-ear piece to 1 outer-ear piece (ensuring the RS of each piece faces outwards) using mattress stitch. Repeat with the remaining ear pieces. Position the ears on the hat using the pictures to guide you, then attach them to the hat. Fold 1 horn piece in half along its length with RS facing in and sew along the edges. Repeat with the other horn piece. Fill the horns with toy filling. Position the horns on the hat using the pictures to guide you, then attach to the hat.

Plaited tassels:

Cut 24 x 90cm/35in strands of yarn D. Align 12 of these and fold them in half. Thread the folded middle of the strands through the gap made by the YO in Row 1 of an earflap to form a little loop. Draw the ends through the loop and pull tight to create a length of 24 strands. Create 3 groups of 8 strands and plait these tightly. Secure the end. Sew 1 pom pom to the end of the tassel. Repeat with the other 12 tassel strands and earflap.

Charts

Template for left earflap

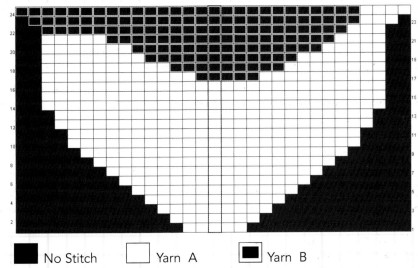

■ No Stitch   □ Yarn A   ■ Yarn B

Template for hat

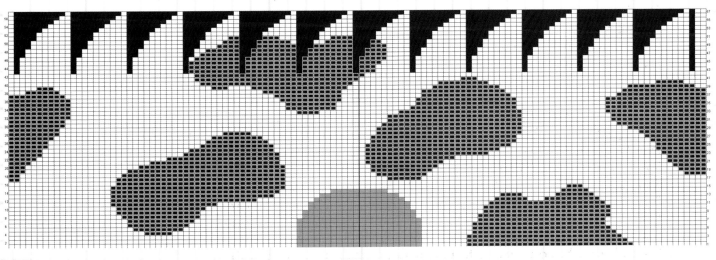

■ No Stitch   □ Yarn A   ■ Yarn B   ▨ Yarn C

CRAB HAT

Benjamin G. Wilson

This cheeky little crab is made using a yummy aran weight alpaca yarn. He's made in an interesting way, as he's worked in the round, knitting every row, but it's the reverse stocking stitch side that is the right side. Very little shaping is required, and the i-cord technique is also used to make this fun, unique beanie.

Size: Adult (one size)

Materials:

~ 1x 50g ball of Rowan Creative Focus Worsted shade 02055, Carmine.
~ Round marker.
~ Stuffing or toy filling.
~ 2 x stitch holders
~ Tapestry needle and short lengths of strong bright red yarn for finishing.
~ 2 x small black domed buttons.

Needles:

~ 1 pair of 4.5mm (US 7) double-pointed needles.
~ 1 pair of 4.5mm (US 7) 40cm/15½in circular needle.

Tension

20sts and 24 rows to 10cm/4in square over st st using 4.5mm (US 7) needles.

Pattern:

Hat:

Using the 4.5mm (US 7) circular needle cast on 92 sts. Place marker at end of row.

First round: *k2, p2 rep from * to end. This row sets the 2 x 2 rib. Work 3 more rounds of 2 x 2 rib.

Change to st st (k each round).

Next round: *k2tog, k44, rep from * to end (90 sts).

Continue in st st until work measures 18cm/7in from cast on edge.

Begin shaping (change to dpns when needed):

Round 1: *k2tog, k16 rep from * to end (85 sts).

Round 2 and every alt round: k to end.

Round 3: *k7, sl1, k2tog, psso, k7 rep from * to end (75 sts).

Round 5: *k6, sl1, k2tog, psso, k6 rep from * to end (65 sts).

Round 7: *k5, sl1, k2tog, psso, k5 rep from * to end (55 sts).

Round 9: *k4, sl1, k2tog, psso, k4 rep from * to end (45 sts).

Round 11: *k3, sl1, k2tog, psso, k3 rep from * to end (35 sts).

Round 13: *k2, sl1, k2tog, psso, k2 rep from * to end (25 sts).

Round 15: *k1, sl1, k2tog, psso, k1 rep from * to end (15 sts).

Round 17: *sl1, k2tog, psso, rep from * to end (5 sts).

Bearing in mind that the k side is the WS, thread the yarn through remaining sts and fasten off securely.

Claws (make 2):

Using 2 x 4.5mm (US 7) dpns, cast on 12 sts.

Row 1: k to end.

Row 2: k1, m1, p4, m1, p2, m1, p4, m1, k1 (16 sts).

Row 3: k1, m1, k6, m1, k2, m1, k6, m1, k1 (20 sts).

Row 4: k1, m1, p8, m1, p2, m1, p8, m1, k1 (24 sts).

Work 6 rows of st st.

Place first and last 3 sts onto separate stitch holders or a scrap of yarn.

Row 1: Using the centre 18 sts, k8, k2tog, k8 (17 sts).

Row 2 and alt rows: p to end.

Row 3: k7, sl1, k2tog, psso, k7 (15 sts).

Row 5: k6, sl1, k2tog, psso, k6 (13 sts).

Row 7: k5, sl1, k2tog, psso, k5 (11 sts).

Cont dec as set until 3 sts remain.

Cast off on WS row.

Place sts on stich holders onto 1 dpn and, using 2 dpns, work 2 rows of i-cord (see page 38).

Row 3: k2tog, k2, k2tog.

Cast off.

Making up:

Weave in all ends.

Block the main body of the hat on a flat surface to eliminate curling.

Sew the side edges of the claws using mattress stitch (see page 22), stuffing the claw lightly as you work.

Using short lengths of bright red yarn, overstitch the black buttons and claws in place, using a mirror and the pictures as a guide.

ZEBRA BEANIE

Sarah Kim

This striking zebra beanie is the ideal project for a more adventurous knitter, and the perfect hat for anyone who likes to be noticed!

Size: Adult (one size)

Materials:

~ Yarn A: 2 x 50g balls of Rowan Pure Wool DK shade 004, Black.
~ Yarn B: 1 x 50g ball of Rowan Pure Wool DK shade 013, Enamel.
~ 2 x black buttons.

Needles:

~ 1 pair of 3.25mm (US 3) needles.
~ 1 pair of 4mm (US 6) needles.

Tension:

22 sts and 30 rows to 10cm/4in square over st st using 4mm needles.

Pattern:

Hat:

Using 3.25mm (US 3) needles and yarn A, cast on 124 sts.
Row 1: *k1, p1, rep from * to end.
This row forms the rib. Cont in rib for 7 more rows, ending with RS facing for next row.

Change to 4mm (US 6) needles. Join yarn B.
Next row: Work across Row 1 of the chart shown on page 81 using yarns A and B, using the intarsia technique (see page 23). Continue to follow the chart until Row 36 of the chart has been completed. (Note that odd-numbered rows should be knitted and even numbered rows should be purled.) End with RS facing for next row.

Begin shaping.

Continuing to follow the chart, working as follows:
Row 37: k1, k2tog, *k8, k2tog, rep from * to last st, k1 (111 sts).
Rows 38–40: Work in st st, starting with a p row.
Row 41: k2, *k7, k2tog, rep from * to last st, k1 (99 sts).
Row 42 and every alt row: p to end.
Row 43: k2, *k6, k2tog, rep from * to last st, k1 (87 sts).
Row 45: k2, *k5, k2tog, rep from * to last st, k1 (75 sts).
Row 47: k2, *k4, k2tog, rep from * to last st, k1 (63 sts).
Row 49: k2, *k3, k2tog, rep from * to last st, k1 (51 sts).
Row 51: k2, *k2, k2tog, rep from * to last st, k1 (39 sts).
Row 53: k2, *k1, k2tog, rep from * to last st, k1 (27 sts).
Row 55: k2, *k2tog, rep from * to last st, k1 (15 sts).
Break off yarn, thread it through the remaining sts and fasten off securely.

Outer ears (make 2):
Using 4mm (US 6) needles and yarn B, cast on 15 sts.
Starting with a k row (RS), work 12 rows in st st.
Row 13: k1, s1, k1, psso, k9, k2tog, k1 (13 sts).
Row 14 and every alt row: p to end.
Row 15: k1, s1, k1, psso, k7, k2tog, k1 (11 sts).
Row 17: k1, s1, k1, psso, k5, k2tog, k1 (9 sts).
Row 19: k1, s1, k1, psso, k3, k2tog, k1 (7 sts).
Row 21: k1, s1, k1, psso, k1, k2tog, k1 (5 sts).
Row 23: k1, s1, k2tog, psso, k1 (3 sts).
Row 24: p3tog.
Break off yarn, thread it through the remaining st and fasten off securely.

Inner ears (make 2):
Using 4mm (US 6) needles and yarn A, cast on 13 sts.
Starting with a k row (RS), work 12 rows in st st.
Row 13: k1, s1, k1, psso, k7, k2tog, k1 (11 sts).
Row 14 and every alt row: p to end.
Row 15: k1, s1, k1, psso, k5, k2tog, k1 (9 sts).
Row 17: k1, s1, k1, psso, k3, k2tog, k1 (7 sts).
Row 19: k1, s1, k1, psso, k1, k2tog, k1 (5 sts).
Row 21: k1, s1, k2tog, psso, k1 (3 sts).
Row 22: p3tog.
Break off yarn, thread it through the remaining st and fasten off securely.

Pom poms (make 4):
Using yarn A, make 4 pom poms (see page 39), each with a 6cm/2½in diameter.

Making up:
Weave in all ends.

Sew the edges of the hat together using mattress stitch (see page 22). The seam marks the centre-back of the hat.

Position the buttons using the pictures to guide you, then sew them on to form eyes.

Sew 1 inner-ear piece to 1 outer-ear piece (ensuring the RS of each piece faces outwards) using mattress stitch. Repeat with the remaining ear pieces.

Position the ears on the hat using the pictures to guide you, then attach them to the hat.

Sew one pom pom to the top of the hat. Attach the other 3 evenly along the back seam of the hat, using the pictures as a guide to their positions.

Chart

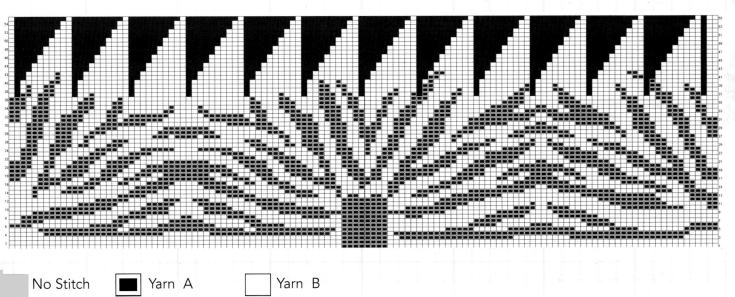

No Stitch ■ Yarn A □ Yarn B

YANG GUANG (PANDA) HAT

Helen Balls

This hat pattern was inspired by one of the latest residents of Edinburgh Zoo! The face details are simple in shape and straightforward to appliqué, yet the effect is striking.

Size: Adult (one size)

Materials:
- Yarn A: 1 x 100g ball of Rowan Creative Focus Worsted shade 500, Ebony.
- Yarn B: 1 x 100g ball of Rowan Pure Wool Aran shade 670, Ivory.
- Black and white felt.
- White card, pencil and paper scissors.
- Tailor's chalk.
- Fabric scissors.

Hook:
- Size 7mm (US 10½) crochet hook.

Tension:
13 stitches and 9 rows to 10cm/4in square measured over treble crochet.

Pattern:
Foundation ring: Using yarn B, work 6ch and join ss to form a ring.

Round 1: ch 3 (counts as 1tr), 11tr into ring, join with ss into third of 3ch (12 sts).

Round 2: ch 3 (counts as 1tr), 1tr into same st, 2tr into each of previous round, join with ss into third of 3ch (24 sts).

Round 3: ch 3 (counts as 1tr), 1tr into same st, [1tr into next tr, 2tr into next tr], rep to last tr, 1tr into last tr, join with ss into third of 3ch (36 sts).

Round 4: ch 3 (counts as 1tr), 1tr into same st, [1tr into each of next 2tr, 2tr into next tr], rep to last 2tr, 1tr into each of next 2tr, join with ss into third of 3ch (48 sts).

Round 5: ch 3 (counts as 1tr), 1tr into same st, [1tr in to each of next 3tr, 2tr into next tr] rep to last 3tr, 1tr into each of next 3tr, join with ss into third of 3ch (60 sts).

Rounds 6–8: ch 3 (counts as 1tr), miss the first tr, 1tr into each remaining tr of previous round, join with ss into third of 3 chain.

Rounds 9–14: ch 3, 1tr into each tr of previous round, join with ss into third of 3 chain.

Eyes and nose:
Using the templates provided on page 84 as your guide, draw the outlines onto a piece of paper and cut them out.
Place the eye template on the black felt and cut it out twice.
Place the smaller nose template on the black felt and cut it out.
Place the larger nose template on the white felt and cut it out.
Position the felt shapes on the front of the hat using the picture opposite to guide you, then attach them to the hat using blanket stitch (see page 37).

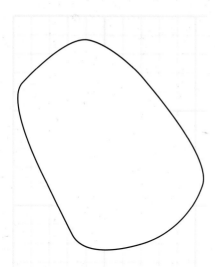

Template for eye

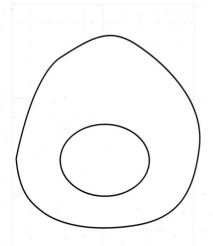

Template for nose

Sew on 2 black buttons as eyes, using the pictures to guide you.

Ears:
Using yarn A, make 2 black pom poms (see page 39), each with a diameter of 6cm/2¼in, ensuring you use a long piece of yarn to tie each pom pom.

Position the ears on the hat using the picture opposite to guide you, then attach the long tails to the hat with a simple knot.

CROCHETED CAT HAT

Rachel Henderson

The pattern for this purrrfect kitty hat is very basic, but the embroidery really brings the cat to life. Kid Classic yarn is a lovely soft choice for this project.

Size: Adult (one size).

Materials:
- 1 x 100g ball of Rowan Kid Classic shade 828, Feather.
- Oddments of sky blue and baby pink wool.
- Dark grey embroidery thread.

Hook:
- Size 4.5mm (US 7) crochet hook.

Tension:
16dc and 16 rows to 10cm/4in square.

Pattern:

Hat:
Make 6ch and ss into first ch to form a ring.
Round 1: 12dc into ring (12sts).
Round 2: [1dc into next st, 2dc into next st] rep around (18 sts).
Round 3: [1dc into next 2 sts, 2dc into next st] rep around (24 sts).
Round 4: [1dc into next 3 sts, 2dc into next st] rep around (30 sts).
Round 5: [1dc into next 4 sts, 2dc into next st] rep around (36 sts).
Round 6: [1dc into next 5 sts, 2dc into next st] rep around (42 sts).

Round 7: [1dc into next 6 sts, 2dc into next st] rep around (48 sts).
Round 8: [1dc into next 7 sts, 2dc into next st] rep around (54 sts).
Round 9: [1dc into next 8 sts, 2dc into next st] rep around (60 sts).
Round 10: [1dc into next 9 sts, 2dc into next st] rep around (66 sts).
Round 11: [1dc into next 10 sts, 2dc into next st] rep around (72 sts).
Round 12: Miss 1dc, 1dc into every following st (71 sts).
Round 13: Miss 1dc, 1dc into every following st (70 sts).
Next few rounds: Work in dc until work measures 18cm/7in.
Fasten off securely.

Earflaps (make 2):
Starting 8 sts in from the centre (both sides) at the bottom of the hat, work 1dc in each of the next 15 sts.
Foundation row: ch1, 1dc in each of the next 15dc.
Row 1: ch1, 1dc, dec1, dc around to last 3 sts, dec1, 1dc (13 sts).
Row 2: ch1, 1dc in each st around.
Row 3: ch1, 1dc, dec1, dc around to last 3 sts, dec1, 1 dc (11 sts).
Row 4: ch1, 1dc in each st around.
Row 5: ch1, 1dc, dec1, dc around to last 3 sts, dec1, 1 dc (9 sts).
Row 6: ch1, 1dc in each st around.
Row 7: ch1, 1dc, dec1, dc around to last 3 sts, dec1, 1 dc (7 sts).
Row 8: ch1, 1dc in each st around.
Row 9: ch1, 1dc, [dec1] x 3 (4 sts).
Row 10: ch1, 1dc, dec1 (3 sts).
Row 11: ch1, 1dc, dec1 (2 sts).
Row 12: dec1 (1 st).
Fasten off securely.

Ears (make 4):
Make 12ch.
Foundation row: ch1, 1dc in each st around.
Row 1: ch1, 1dc, dec1, dc around to last 3 sts, dec1, 1dc (10 sts).

Row 2: ch1, 1dc in each st around.
Row 3: ch1, 1dc, dec1, dc around to last 3 sts, dec1, 1dc (8 sts).
Row 4: ch1, 1dc in each st around.
Row 5: ch1, 1dc, dec1, dc around to last 3 sts, dec1, 1dc (6 sts).
Row 6: ch1, 1dc in each st around.
Row 7: ch1, 1dc, [dec1] twice, 1 dc (4 sts).
Row 8: ch1, [dec1] x 2 (2 sts).
Fasten off securely.

Cheeks (make 2):
Make 4ch using pink yarn, ss into first ch to form ring.
Round 1: ch1, 6dc into ring, ss into top of ch to join (6 sts).
Round 2: ch1, 2dc into each dc around, ss into top of ch to join (12 sts).
Round 3: ch1, [1dc into next st, 2 dc into next st], rep around, ss into top of ch to join (18 sts).
Round 4: ch1, [1dc into next 2sts, 2 dc into next st], rep around, ss into top of ch to join (24 sts).
Fasten off securely.

Plaits (make 2):
Make long chains using 6 x 1m/1 yard tails.
Plait 3 chain tails together.

Pom poms:
Using pink yarn, make 2 pom poms (see page 39), each with an 8cm/3¼in diameter.

Making up:
Embroider the eyes, nose and whiskers in back and satin stitches (see page 37), using the photograph opposite to guide you on their positions and colours. Sew the cheeks onto each sides of the hat, behind the whiskers, using pink yarn. Pair up 2 ear pieces and sew them together using an overstitch or the slip-stitch method. Repeat with the other 2 ear pieces. Position the ears on the hat using the photographs to guide you, then sew them onto the hat. Attach 1 pom pom to the end of each plait.

KOALA BEAR HAT

Charlotte Pyrah

This simple crocheted hat design is embellished with cute felt koala ears, a simple crocheted nose and eyes and with decorative pom poms. Add furry texture - and a bit of sparkle - to the ears with some Angelina fibres.

Size: Adult (one size)

Materials:

- ~ Yarn A: 1 x 50g ball of Rowan Cotton Glace shade 843, Toffee.
- ~ Yarn B: 2 x 50g balls of Rowan Cotton Glace shade 831, Dawn Grey.
- ~ Yarn C: 1 x 50g ball of Rowan Cotton Glace shade 737, Black.
- ~ White card, pencil and paper scissors.
- ~ Black felt.
- ~ White felt.
- ~ Tailor's chalk.
- ~ Fabric scissors.
- ~ Heat bondable Angelina fibres in Crystal, Mother of Pearl and Emerald Flash. You'll need a 10gms bag of each.
- ~ Bondaweb.

Crochet hook:

- ~ 4.5mm (US 7).
- ~ 3.5mm (US 4/E).

Tension:

22 stitches and 9 rows to 10cm/4in square measured over half treble crochet.

Pattern:

Using yarn B and the 4.5mm (US 7) hook, ch90. ss into first ch to form a ring.

Round 1: ch1 (counts as first dc), 1dc into each st to end of round. ss into first ch to join.

Rounds 2–5: As round 1.

Round 6: ch2 (counts as first htr), 1htr into each st to end of round. ss into second of 2ch to join.

Rounds 7–13: As round 6.

Round 14: ch2 (counts as first htr), 1htr into each st to end of round. ss into second of 2ch to join.

Round 15: ch2 (counts as first htr), 1htr into each of next 6sts, dec1, *[1htr into each of next 7 sts, dec1], rep from * to end of round. ss into second of 2ch to join (80 sts).

Round 16: ch2 (counts as first htr), 1htr into each of next 5 sts, dec1, *[1htr into each of next 6sts, dec1], rep from * to end of round. ss into second of 2ch to join (70 sts).

Round 17: ch2 (counts as first htr), 1htr into each of next 4 sts, dec1, *[1htr into each of next 5 sts, dec1], rep from * to end of round. ss into second of 2ch to join (60 sts).

Round 18: ch2 (counts as first htr), 1htr into each of next 3 sts, dec1, *[1htr into each of next 4 sts, dec1], rep from * to end of round. ss into second of 2ch to join (50 sts).

Round 19: ch2 (counts as first htr), 1htr into each of next 2 sts, dec1, *[1htr into each of next 3 sts, dec1], rep from * to end of round. ss into second of 2ch to join (40 sts).

Round 20: ch2 (counts as first htr), 1htr into next st, dec1, *[1htr into each of next 2 sts, dec1], rep from * to end of round. ss into second of 2ch to join (30 sts).

Round 21: ch2 (counts as first htr), dec1, *[1htr into next st, dec1], rep from * to end of round. ss into second of 2ch to join (20 sts).

Round 22: ch2 (counts as first htr), dec1. Repeat to end of round. ss into second of 2ch to join. Fasten off securely, leaving a small length of yarn. Draw the yarn through remaining sts and sew up the gap.

Inner ears (make 2):
Using yarn B and 3.5mm (US 4/E) hook, ch5. ss into first ch to form ring.
Round 1: ch1, 6dc into ring, ss into top of ch to join (6 sts).
Round 2: ch2, 2dc into each st around. ss into second of 2ch to join (12 sts).
Round 3: ch3, 2htr into each st around. ss into third of 3ch to join (24 sts).
Round 4: ch3, *[1tr into next st, 2tr into next st], rep from * to end of round, ss into third of ch to join (36 sts).
Fasten off securely.

Outer ears:
Trace the template shown opposite onto card and cut it out. On the white felt, trace around the ear template 4 times using tailor's chalk. On the Bondaweb, trace around it 2 times. Cut out each piece. Using an iron, bond 2 pieces of felt together using bondaweb between them to stiffen. Repeat with the other 2 outer-ear pieces and piece of bondaweb. Double thread a large-eyed needle with yarn B and around edge of each felt ear work lots of loopy stitches which are 6cm in length. Repeat with yarn A. Arrange a really thin, whispy layer of Angelina fibres (both shades) across the front and around the edge of each felt ear. Place a piece of greaseproof paper on top of and iron across for a few seconds to fix them. Stitch the crocheted inner ears onto the centre of each front felt ear using an overstitch. Position the ears on the hat using the pictures to guide you, then attach them to the hat using an overstitch.

Nose:
Using yarn C, follow the instructions for making the inner ear. Position the nose on the hat using the pictures to guide you, then attach it to the hat using overstitch.

Eyes (make 2):
Using 3.5mm (US 4/E) hook and yarn C, ch5. ss into first ch to form ring.
Round 1: Work 12dc into the ring.
Round 2: Work 1dc in each st around. ss into first dc to join.
Fasten off securely.
Position the eyes on the hat using the pictures to guide you, then attach them to the hat using overstitch.

Cords:
Cut 10 x 1m/1 yard lengths of yarn B.
Cut 10 x 1m/1 yard lengths of yarn A.
To create a twisted cord take 5 lengths of yarn A and 5 lengths of yarn B and tie all the pieces together loosely at one end. Place around either a post on a chair or a door knob, separating out your two shades. Start to twist together, carrying the left section of strands over the right. Continue to do so making sure you always twist in the same direction. When you have finished, remove the cord keeping hold of both ends of the yarn and let it unfold slightly. Tie a knot at the bottom to secure. Repeat with the remaining yarn lengths to create a second cord.

Make 2 x 6cm/2¼in pom poms (see page 39) using yarns A and B together and some thin whisps of Angelina fibres (both shades). Attach one pom pom to the end of each twisted cord. Stitch a cord onto the hat behind each ear.

Template for outer ear

3

*Babies &
Toddlers*

FLEECE FROG

Rachel Henderson

This charming frog's earflap legs will help to keep kids warm as they leap about outdoors in cold weather. Use a fleece in a nice and bright shade of pale green, so you can spot your little hopper in the distance! Mr Frog likes to be worn by boys and girls alike.

Sizes and dimensions:

0–6 months: 41cm/16in circumference.

6–12 months: 44cm/17in circumference.

1–3 years: 47cm/18½in circumference.

3–5 years: 49cm/19in circumference.

Materials:

~ White card, pencil and paper scissors.

~ 75cm/1½ yards pale green fleece.

~ Tailor's chalk.

~ Fabric scissors.

~ Pins.

~ Sewing machine (optional).

~ Scraps of white and brown or black fleece/felt.

~ Pale green cotton sewing thread.

~ Black embroidery thread.

Working an overstitch:

Overstitches are a series of widely or closely set zig-zag stitches worked in a line to join one edge of fabric to another.

How to make:

Step 1: Using pattern diagrams 1 and 2, create card pattern pieces to the dimensions provided. Place pattern 1 (band with earflaps) onto the green fleece and trace around it twice using tailor's chalk. Place pattern 2 (hat top) onto the wrong side of the fleece and trace around it 4 times using tailor's chalk. Cut out all the pieces for the hat top and earflaps.

Step 2: Align the earflap fleece sections with their RS facing in. Using a 1cm/⅜in seam allowance, machine or hand stitch around the earflaps, leaving the top and sides of the band open. Turn the RS to face out.

Step 3: Pin the top fleece sections together at the side edges with WS facing in. Using a 1cm/⅜in seam allowance, stitch down each section.

Step 4: Pin the edge of the top fleece sections to the top band with WS facing in, ensuring they are aligned. Using a 1cm/3/8in seam allowance, stitch across.

Step 5: Pin together the back seams and stitch across the top hat sections and band side edges to join together.

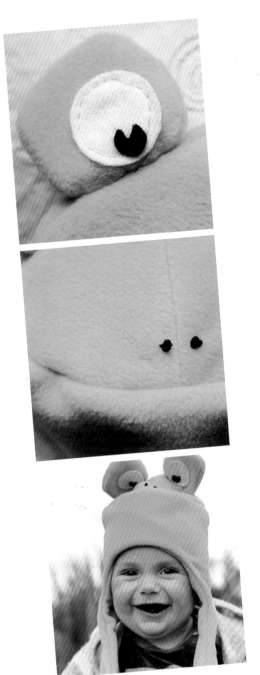

Step 6:
Trace templates 1, 2 and 3 onto white card and cut out. Place template 1 (outer eye) onto the green fleece and trace the outline 4 times using tailor's chalk. Place template 2 (inner eye 1) onto the white felt and trace the outline twice using tailor's chalk. Place template 3 (inner-eye 2) onto the brown or black felt and trace the outline twice using tailor's chalk. Cut out the pieces for the inner and outer eyes. Position 1 smaller inner eye (brown or black felt) onto on 1 larger inner eye (white felt), and stitch to attach, using the pictures to guide you. Then attach the larger inner eye (white felt) to 1 outer eye (green fleece) by working a backstitch around edge. Repeat with the other eye pieces.

Step 7: Place 2 outer eyes shapes together – 1 with an inner eye attached, 1 without – so that the RS are facing each other and stitch around, leaving a small gap at the centre bottom edge for folding outwards. Turn the RS to face out. Repeat with the remaining eye shapes.

Step 8: Stitch up the gaps at the bottom of the outer eye shapes. Position the eyes on the hat using the pictures to guide you, then attach them to the hat using an overstitch.

Step 9: Embroider the nose with the black thread using French knot stitch (see below).

French knot stitch:
Take the working thread through to the front of your fabric. Make a small loop of thread and hold this with your left thumb. Encircle the thread three times (or more if you want to achieve a larger knot) around the needle. Position the needle so that it sits close to where you pulled the thread through. Take the needle from the front to the back of the fabric, leaving a small knot on the surface.

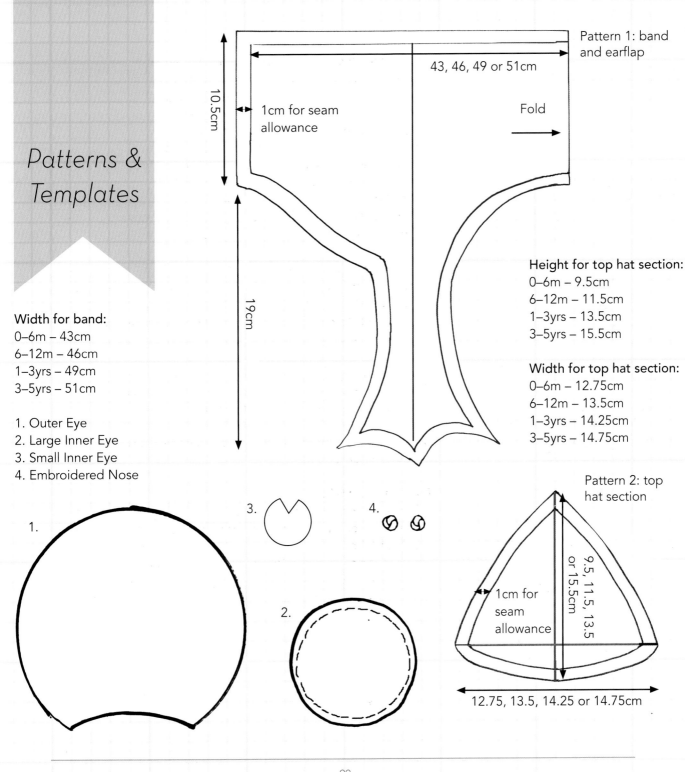

Patterns & Templates

Pattern 1: band and earflap

10.5cm

43, 46, 49 or 51cm

1cm for seam allowance

Fold

19cm

Height for top hat section:
0–6m – 9.5cm
6–12m – 11.5cm
1–3yrs – 13.5cm
3–5yrs – 15.5cm

Width for top hat section:
0–6m – 12.75cm
6–12m – 13.5cm
1–3yrs – 14.25cm
3–5yrs – 14.75cm

Width for band:
0–6m – 43cm
6–12m – 46cm
1–3yrs – 49cm
3–5yrs – 51cm

1. Outer Eye
2. Large Inner Eye
3. Small Inner Eye
4. Embroidered Nose

1.

3.

4.

2.

Pattern 2: top hat section

9.5, 11.5, 13.5 or 15.5cm

1cm for seam allowance

12.75, 13.5, 14.25 or 14.75cm

FLEECE FISH HAT

Rachel Henderson

Meet Fred the fish, who loves to pout at all the boys and girls! This characterful hat is so eye catching, it's sure to draw a crowd of playmates in the playground. A tied top makes an excellent tail for Fred in this funky fleece beanie.

Sizes and dimensions:

0–6 months: 41cm/16in circumference.

6–12 months: 44cm/17in circumference.

1–3 years: 47cm/18½in circumference.

3–5 years: 49cm/19in circumference

Materials needed

~ White card, pencil and paper scissors.
~ 75cm/½ yard pale blue fleece.
~ Large scraps of dark pink, pale pink, mid blue, white and black felt.
~ Tailor's chalk.
~ Fabric scissors.
~ Pins.
~ Blue cotton sewing thread.
~ Blue embroidery thread.
~ Sewing machine (optional).
~ Stuffing or toy filling.
~ Fabric glue.

How to make:

Step 1: Using the pattern diagram (see page 103), create a card pattern piece for the main hat using the dimensions provided. Place the pattern piece onto the wrong side of the blue fleece, trace around twice using tailor's chalk and cut out the shapes for the front and back of the hat. Fold over the bottom edge of each piece by 6cm/2½in on the wrong side and pin in place to form a hem. Now mark out a dart on the wrong side of the fabric and the centre-top. This dart should be 2cm/¾in wide and 14cm/5½in deep. Pin the darts, ready for sewing. Using the blue cotton thread, stitch across both hems and sew across the darts on each piece, using either a sewing machine or working by hand.

Step 2: To make the pouty mouth, fold a 13cm x 7cm (5in x 2¾in) strip of dark pink felt in half along its length with the RS facing in. Sew along the edges using a sewing machine, leaving a gap of 3cm/1¼in. Turn the RS out through the gap you left, then stuff the tube with toy filling. Now stitch the 2 ends of the tube together to form a circle. Attach this to the RS of the front piece of the hat using fabric glue. Use the picture opposite as a guide when positioning the mouth.

Step 3: Trace templates 1, 2 and 3 onto white card for eyes and spots, and cut out. Use template 4 to create a card pattern piece for the water using the dimensions provided. Place template 1 (outer eye) onto the white felt and trace the outline twice using tailor's chalk. Place template 2 (inner eye 1) onto the black felt and and trace the outline twice using tailor's chalk. Do the same for template 3 on pink felt and template 4 on light blue felt. Cut out all the shapes.

Step 4: Place 1 inner eye shape onto the centre of each outer eye shape and attach with fabric glue. Position the assembled eye shapes on the front of the hat (using the pictures to guide you) and, using blue cotton sewing thread, attach with a blanket stitch (see page 37)

Step 5: Align the 2 hat pieces with their RS facing in and, working with a 1cm/⅜in seam allowance, stitch the sides together, leaving the bottom and top ends of the hat open. Turn the RS to face out, then, working roughly 7cm down from top of hat (front and back), tie a piece of blue embroidery thread around this section so that there is no gap at top of hat anymore. Secure with a double knot and cut the thread ends.

Step 6: Use template 5 to create a card pattern piece for the fins using the dimensions provided. Place your card template onto the pale blue fleece, trace the outline 4 times using tailor's chalk then cut out the pieces. Take 2 fin shapes and align them with the RS facing in. Stitch the edges using a 5mm/³⁄₁₆in seam allowance, leaving a 3cm/2½in gap along the straight edge. Repeat with the other 2 fin pieces.

Step 7: Turn each of the fins RS facing out through the gap you left, then stuff with toy filling and stitch up the gap using blue cotton thread. Hand-stitch the fins to the sides of the hat using an overstitch.

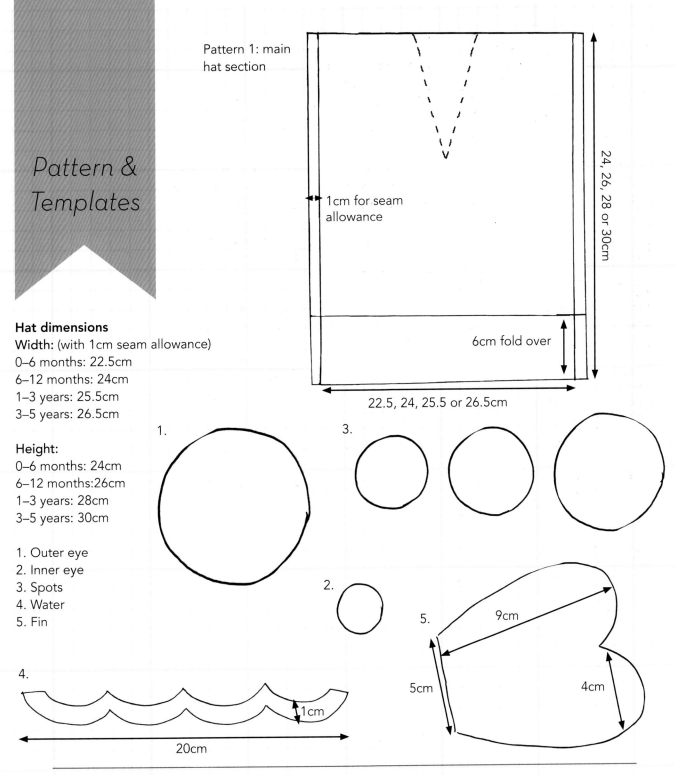

Pattern & Templates

Pattern 1: main hat section

1cm for seam allowance

24, 26, 28 or 30cm

6cm fold over

22.5, 24, 25.5 or 26.5cm

Hat dimensions

Width: (with 1cm seam allowance)
0–6 months: 22.5cm
6–12 months: 24cm
1–3 years: 25.5cm
3–5 years: 26.5cm

Height:
0–6 months: 24cm
6–12 months: 26cm
1–3 years: 28cm
3–5 years: 30cm

1. Outer eye
2. Inner eye
3. Spots
4. Water
5. Fin

1.

3.

2.

5.

9cm

5cm

4cm

4.

1cm

20cm

FLEECE MOUSE HAT

Rachel Henderson

Fleecy mouse's adorable pink pom pom nose and big ears make him very cute. The mouth and whiskers are fun to embroider.

Sizes and dimensions

0–6 months: 41cm/16in circumference.

6–12 months: 44cm/17in circumference.

1–3 years: 47cm/18½in circumference.

3–5 years: 49cm/19in circumference.

Materials:

~ White card, pencil and paper scissors.

~ 25cm/10in pale grey fleece.

~ Tailor's chalk.

~ Fabric scissors.

~ Pins.

~ Sewing machine (optional).

~ Scraps of white fleece/felt.

~ 2 x black buttons.

~ Grey cotton sewing thread.

~ White cotton sewing thread.

~ Black embroidery thread.

~ Baby pink yarn.

How to make:

Step 1: Using the pattern diagram (see page 107), create a card pattern piece for the main hat using the dimensions provided. Place the pattern piece onto the wrong side of the grey fleece, trace around twice using tailor's chalk and cut out the shapes for the front and back of the hat.

Step 2: Fold over the bottom edge of each piece by 6cm/2½in on the WS and pin in place to form a hem. Mark out a 2cm/¾in (width) by 6cm/2¼ (deep) dart at the centre-top of both fleece shapes on the WS. Pin the darts, ready for sewing. Stitch across both hems using a straight stitch. Sew across each using either a sewing machine or working by hand.

Step 4: Add whiskers and a mouth to the front hat shape using backstitch (see page 37), using the pictures to guide you. Position the buttons as eyes and stitch them on using the white sewing thread. Make a pom pom (see page 39) with a diameter of 4cm/1½in and sew this in place for a nose.

Step 5: Align the main hat pieces with RS facing in. Working with a 1cm/⅜in seam allowance, stitch the hat pieces together, leaving the bottom edge open.

Step 6: Turn the RS out. Trace templates 1 and 2 (outer and inner ears) onto white card and cut out. Place template 1 (inner ears) onto the white felt and trace the outline twice. Place template 2 (outer ears) onto the grey fleece and trace the outline four times. Cut out the outer and inner ear pieces.

Step 7: Position 1 inner-ear shape on each outer-ear shape, using the pictures to guide you, then, using black emroidery thread, attach to the centre with backstitch (see page 37). Align 1 outer-ear piece that has an inner-ear piece attached to it with a plain outer-ear piece with their RS facing in. Using a 5mm/³⁄₁₆in seam allowance, stitch around from the left edge to the right edge, leaving the bottom open.

Step 8: Turn the ears RS facing out and stitch up the opening using cotton thread. Position the ears on the hat using the pictures to guide you, then attach them to the hat using an overstitch.

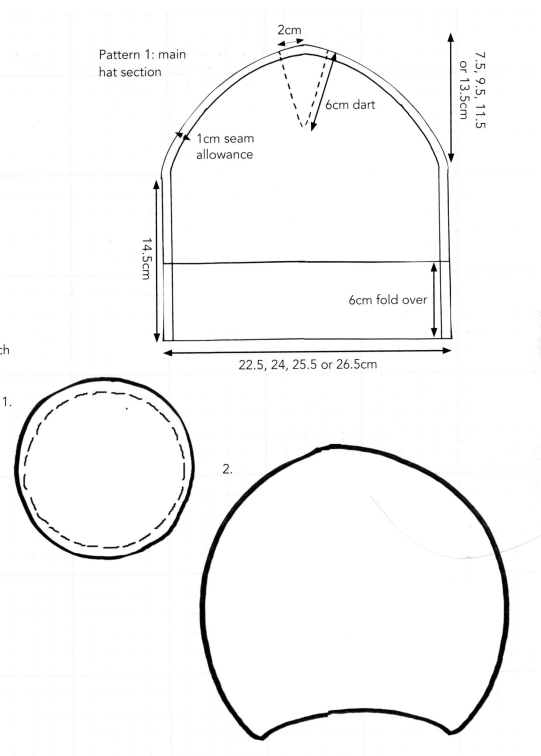

Pattern & Templates

Hat dimensions

Width: (with 1cm/⅜in at each edge for seam allowance)
0–6 months: 22.5cm
6–12 months: 24cm
1–3 years: 25.5cm
3–5 years: 26.5cm

Height for band and fold-over section: 14.5cm

Height for top:
0–6 months: 7.5cm/3in
6–12 months: 9.5cm/3¾in
1–3 years: 11.5cm/4½in
3–5 years: 13.5cm/5¼in

1. Inner ear
2. Outer ear

Pattern 1: main hat section

2cm

6cm dart

1cm seam allowance

7.5, 9.5, 11.5 or 13.5cm

14.5cm

6cm fold over

22.5, 24, 25.5 or 26.5cm

1.

2.

CROCHETED LADYBIRD HAT

Rachel Henderson

This sweet little ladybird hat makes an excellent gift for a girl. The spots are created with spiralled lengths of chain stitches, and huge woolly pom poms are lots of fun! The earflaps will ensure those little ears are kept nice and cosy.

Sizes:
0–6 months: 41cm/16in
6–12 months: 44cm/17½in
1–3 years: 47cm/18½in
3–5 years: 49cm/19½in

Materials:
~ Yarn A: 1 x 50g ball Rowan Cashsoft DK shade 519, Black.
~ Yarn B: 1 x 50g ball Rowan Cashsoft DK shade 512, Poppy.
~ White felt.
~ 2 x small black buttons.

Crochet hook:
~ Size 3.5mm (US 4E) crochet hook.

Tension:
18dcs x 18 rows to 10cm/4in square.

Pattern:
All sizes:
Using yarn A, ch6. ss into first ch to form a ring.
Round 1: work 12dc into ring (12 sts).
Round 2: [1dc into next st, 2dc into next st] rep around (18 sts).
Round 3: [1dc into next 2 sts, 2dc into next st], rep around (24 sts).
Round 4: [1dc into next 3 sts, 2dc into next st], rep around (30 sts).
Round 5: [1dc into next 4 sts, 2dc into next st], rep around (36 sts).
Round 6: [1dc into next 5 sts, 2dc into next st], rep around (42 sts).
Round 7: [1dc into next 6 sts, 2dc into next st], rep around (48 sts).
Round 8: [1dc into next 7 sts, 2dc into next st], rep around (54 sts).
Round 9: [1dc into next 8 sts, 2dc into next st], rep around (60 sts).
Round 10: [1dc into next 9 sts, 2dc into next st], rep around (66 sts).
Round 11: [1dc into next 10 sts, 2dc into next st], rep around (72 sts).

Sizes 6–12 months, 1–3 years and 3–5 years only:
Round 12: [1dc into next 11 sts, 2dc into next st], rep around (78 sts).

Sizes 1–3 years and 3–5 years only:
Round 13: [1dc into next 12 sts, 2dc into next st], rep around (84 sts).

Size 3–5 years only:
Round 14: [1dc into next 13 sts, 2dc into next st], rep around (90 sts).

All sizes:
Next round: Miss 1dc, 1dc into each st around (71 (77, 83, 89) sts).
Next round: Miss 1dc, 1dc into each st around 70 (76, 82, 88) sts).

Work 2 more rounds in yarn A working 1dc in each st around. Change to yarn B. Continue to work in dc until hat measures

15cm/6in (16cm/6¼in, 17cm/6½, 18cm/7in).
Fasten off securely.

Earflaps:

Using Yarn B, and starting 6 (7, 8, 9) sts in from bottom-centre of the hat (both sides), work 1dc in each of next 13 (13, 15, 15) sts.
Foundation row: Ch1, 1dc in each st across. 13 (13:15:15) sts
Row 1: ch1, 1dc in each st across.
Row 2: ch1, 1dc, dec1, dc across to last 3 sts, dec1, 1dc (11 (11, 13, 13) sts).
Row 3: ch1, 1dc in each st across.
Row 4: ch1, 1dc, dec1, dc across to last 3 sts, dec1, 1dc (9 (9, 11, 11) sts).
Row 5: ch1, 1dc in each st across.
Row 6: ch1, 1dc, dec1, dc across to last 3 sts, dec1, 1dc (7 (7, 9, 9) sts).
Row 7: ch1, 1dc in each st across.

Sizes 1–3 years and 3–5 years only:

Repeat rows 6 & 7 once more (7 (7) sts).

Next row: ch1, 1dc, [dec1] x 3 (4 sts).
Next row: ch1, 1dc, dec1, 1dc (3 sts).
Next row: ch1, 1dc, dec1 (2sts).
Next row: ch1, dec1 (1st).
Fasten off securely.

Small spots (make 6):

Using yarn A, ch25 and then fasten off securely.

Large spots (make 4):

Using yarn A, ch35 and then fasten off securely.

Antennae (make 2):

Using yarn A, ch5. ss into first ch to form a ring.
Round 1: ch1, 1dc into each st around (5 sts).
Rounds 2–3: As round 1.
Round 4: ch1, 1dc in next st, dec1, 1dc in each of next 2 sts (4 sts).
Rounds 5–6: ch1, 1dc into each st around
Round 7: ch1, 1dc in next st, dec1, 1dc in next st (3 sts).
Rounds 8–9: ch1, 1dc into each st around.
Round 10: ch1, 1dc, dec1 (2 sts).
Rounds 11–12: ch1, 1dc into each st around.
Fasten off securely.

Eyes (make 2):

Using the template opposite as a guide, draw the shape onto white card and cut it out. Pin it onto the white felt, draw around it twice and cut out the eye shapes.

Making up:

Coil up the lengths of chain sts to create spots. Position these on the hat using the picture opposite to guide you, then attach them to the hat, either by using fabric glue or by hand sewing using cotton thread.

Position the antennae on the top-back of the hat using the picture opposite to guide you, then attach them to hat using an overstitch.

Using yarn A, make 2 x 12cm/4½in pom poms (see page 39). Attach one to the end of each earflap.

Template for eye

KNITTED LAMB BONNET

Rachel Henderson

Perfect for any adorable little lambs you know, this hat is made using a gorgeous bobbly wool that gives the effect of a lamb's cuddly coat. The pink knitted cord, which ties in a bow, adds another sweet touch.

Sizes and dimensions:
0–6 months: 41cm/16in circumference.
6–12 months: 44cm/17½in circumference.
1–3 years: 47cm/18½in circumference.
3–5 years: 49cm/19½in circumference.

Materials:
~ Yarn A: 1 x 100g ball of Rowan British Sheep Breeds Bouclé shade 00220, Ecru.
~ Yarn B: 1 x 50g ball RYC Cashsoft DK shade 00540, Sky Pink.

Needles:
~ 1 pair of 4mm (US 6) needles.
~ 1 pair of 8mm (US 11) needles.

Tension:
8.5 sts and 13 rows to 10cm/4in square over stocking stitch using 8mm (US 11) needles.

Pattern:
Top and side panels:
Using 8mm (US 11) needles and yarn A, cast on 32 (34, 38, 40) sts.
Work 2 rows in moss stitch as follows:
Row 1: *k1, p1, rep from * to end.
Row 2: *p1, k1, rep from * to end.
Change to stocking stitch and continue straight until work measures 12cm/4½in (12.5cm/4¾in, 13.5cm/5¼in, 14.5cm/5¾in) from cast on edge, ending with a p row.
Next row: Cast off 10 (11, 12, 13) sts, k12 (12, 14, 14), cast off 10 (11, 12, 13) sts. You should have 12 stitches on your needle. Break off yarn.

Back panel:
With WS facing, re-join yarn to remaining sts and p 1 row.
Cont in stocking stitch until work measures 11cm/4¼in (11.5cm/4½in, 12.5cm/4¾in, 13.5cm/5¼in).
Cast off.

Using mattress stitch, join back panel edges to 10 (11, 12, 13) cast off sts of right and left sides panels of bonnet.

Neck trim:
With RS facing, pick up 8 (9, 9, 10) sts evenly along left side panel, 12 (12, 14, 14) sts from back panel and 8 (9, 9, 10) sts evenly from side panel (28 (30, 32, 34) sts).
Work 2 rows in moss stitch.
Cast off.

Ears (make 2):

Using yarn A using 8mm (US 11) needles and 2 in yarn B using 4mm (US 6) needles):

Cast on 7 sts.

Rows 1–5: *k1, p1, rep from * to end.

Row 6: p2tog, k1, p1, k1, p2tog.

Row 7: p1, k1, p1, k1, p1.

Row 8: k2tog, p1, k2tog.

Row 9: k3tog.

Break off yarn, thread it through the remaining st and fasten off.

Tie (make 2):

Using 4mm (US 6) needles and yarn B, cast on 7 sts.

Work in moss stitch as follows:

Row 1: *k1, p1, rep from * to last st, k1.

Row 2: as row 1.

Continue in moss stitch for 26cm/10in.

Cast off.

Pom poms:

Using yarn A, make 2 pom poms (see page 39), each with a diameter of 4cm/1½in.

Making up:

Pin 1 inner-ear piece to 1 outer-ear piece, easing the outer ear to fit around the inner ear. Stitch together using an overstitch with RS facing out. Repeat with the remaining ear pieces.

Fold 1 ear in half lengthwise, so that the inner ear is innermost, and oversew the cast on edge to secure the fold. Repeat with the other ear.

Position the ears on the hat above the start of the seams, using the pictures to guide you, then attach them to the hat using an overstitch.

Attach a tie to the bottom left edge of hat using an overstitch, and repeat on the bottom right edge. Attach 1 pom pom to the end of each tie.

KNITTED LION HAT WITH EARFLAPS

Rachel Henderson

Wrarrrr! This bright and cheerful lion hat is perfect for courageous, adventurous and cuddly young souls, and boys seem particularly drawn to it. The mane effect is created by making looped stitches that are then cut open and brushed out. Using a chunky merino wool makes this hat lovely and cosy to wear.

Sizes and dimensions:
6–10 years: 50cm/19½in circumference.

Materials:
~ Yarn A: 2 x 100g balls of Rowan Big Wool shade 051, Burnt Orange.
~ Yarn B: 1 x 50g ball of Rowan Big Wool shade 048, Linen.
~ Oddment of black yarn

Needles:
~ 1 pair of 10mm (US 15) needles.

Tension:
8.5sts and 13 rows to 10cm/4in square over st st.

Creating a loop stitch (L1):
Insert your right needle through the next stitch on your left needle as if to knit. Place your left thumb on your left needle. Carry the working yarn between both needles and to the front of the work. Then carry it around your left thumb clockwise and back between the needles to the back of the work, creating a loop. Now insert your right needle down through the top of the first loop of the right needle, knitting the stitch. You now have 2 sts on the right needle knitted from the same st. Using your left needle, carry the second st on your right needle over the first st and off the needle.

Pattern:
Hat:
Using yarn A, cast on 42 sts.
Row 1: *k1, p1, rep from * to end.
Row 2: *pl, k1, rep from * to end.
Row 3: (k1, L1) x 8, k10, (k1, L1) x 8.
Rows 4–6: Work in st st, starting with a p row.
Row 7: (L1, k1) x 8, k10, (L1, k1) x 8.
Rows 8–10: Work in st st, starting with a p row.
Row 11: Work as row 3.
Rows 12–14: Work in st st, starting with a p row.
Row 15: Work as row 7.
Row 16: p to end.
Row 17: k to end.
Begin shaping.
Row 18: *p5, p2tog, rep from * to end (36 sts).
Row 19: *L1, k1, rep from * to end.
Row 20: *p4, p2tog, rep from * to end (30 sts).
Row 21: k to end.
Row 22: *p3, p2tog, rep from * to end (24 sts).
Row 23: *k1, L1, rep from * to end.
Row 254: *p2, p2tog, rep from * to end (18 sts).
Row 265: k to end.
Row 276: *p1, p2tog, rep from * to end (12 sts).
Row 217: k to end.

Row 228: *p2tog, rep from * to end (6sts).
Break off yarn, thread it through the remaining sts and fasten off securely. Sew the side edges of the hat using mattress stitch (see page 22). The seam marks the centre-back of the hat.

Left earflap:

With RS facing, starting at the back seam of the hat, count 5 sts to the left along the cast on edge. From this point, and continuing away from the seam along the cast on edge using yarn A, pick up and k 10 sts.
Row 1: p1, k1, p to last 2 sts, k1, p1.
Row 2: p1, k1, k to last 2 sts, k1, p1.
Row 3: p1, k1, p2tog, p2, p2tog, k1, p1.
Row 4: p1, k1, k to last 2 sts, k1, p1.
Row 5: p1, K1, p to last 2 sts k1, p1.
Row 6: p1, k1, k to last 2 sts, k1, p1.
Row 7: p1, k1, p2tog X 2, k1, p1.
Row 8: p1, k1, k to last 2 sts, k1, p1.
Row 9: p1, k1, p2, k1, p1.
Row 10: p1, k1, k2, k1, p1.
Row 11: p1, k1, p2tog, k1, p1.
Row 12: p1, k1, p1, k1, p1. Cast off.

Right earflap:

With RS facing, starting at the back seam of the hat, count 15 sts to the right along the cast on edge. From this point, working back towards the seam along the cast on edge, and using yarn A, pick up and k 10 sts. Work to match the left earflap.

Knitted mouth:

Using yarn B, cast on 11 sts.
Row 1: k to end.
Row 2: p2tog, p to last 2 sts, p2tog.
Row 3: k to end.
Row 4: p to end.
Row 5: k to end.
Row 6: p2tog, p to last 2 sts, p2tog.
Row 7: k3tog, k1, k3tog. Cast off.

Outer ears (make 4):

Using yarn A, cast on 6 sts.
Work in st st for 4 rows, starting with a k row.
Row 5: k2tog, k2, k2tog.
Row 6: p to end.
Row 7: k2tog x 2.
Break off yarn, thread it through the remaining sts and fasten off securely.

Inner ears (make 2):

Using yarn B, cast on 4 sts.
Work in st st for 4 rows, starting with a k row.
Row 5: k2tog x 2.
Break off yarn, thread it through the remaining sts and fasten off securely.

Plaited tassels:

Make 2 plaits using 6 x 25cm/10in strands of yarn B for each plait. Tie together all lengths at top and secure with a knot. Plait all of the yarn strands, tie bottom ends and secure with a knot.

Pom pom (make 2):

Using yarn A, make 2 pom poms (see page 39), each with a 6cm/2½in diameter.

Making up:

Weave in all ends. Pair up 2 outer-ear pieces with WS facing and join the side edges together using an overstitch. Sew 1 inner-ear piece to 1 outer-ear pair with WS facing in. Repeat with the remaining ear pieces. Position the ears on the hat using the picture opposite to guide you, then attach them to the hat. Sew the mouth to the lower face, using the picture opposite to guide you, then embroider the nose and mouth details using black yarn. Using a satin and chain stitch (see page 37), embroider the eyes in black yarn. Cut open all the loops on the hat, tie each in a knot, then brush out the loose yarn. Sew the plaited tassel to the bottom of each earflap using an overstitch. Attach a pom pom to end of each plaited tassel.

KNITTED DINO HAT

Rachel Henderson

This cute dinosaur hat is knitted in a yarn that's made of a wool-cotton blend, so it is great for both winter and summer wear. Although it looks rather spectacular, it is actually quite easy to make!

Size: 6–10 years: 50cm/19½in circumference.

Materials needed:
~ Yarn A: 2 x 50g balls of Rowan Wool Cotton DK, shade 00946, Elf.
~ Yarn B: 1 x 50g ball of Rowan Amy Butler Belle Organic DK, shade 020, Clementine.
~ Yarn C: 1 x 50g ball of Cashsoft DK, shade 509, Lime.
~ White card, pencil and paper scissors.
~ Piece of white felt.
~ Pinking shears.
~ 2 x black buttons.

Needles:
~ 1 pair of 4mm (US 8) needles.

Tension:
22 stitches and 30 rows to 10cm/4in square over st st.

Pattern:
Using yarn A, cast on 100 sts.
Row 1: *k2, p2, rep from * to end.
Repeat Row 1 5 more times.
Next row: k to end.
Next row: p to end.
Continue straight in st st until work measures 11cm/4½in. Begin shaping.
Row 1: *k8, k2tog, rep from * to end (90 sts).
Row 2: and every alt row: p to end.
Row 3: *k7, k2tog, rep from * to end.
Row 5: *k6, k2tog, rep from * to end.
Row 7: *k5, k2tog, rep from * to end.
Row 9: *k4, k2tog, rep from * to end.
Row 11: *k3, k2tog, rep from * to end.
Row 13: *k2, k2tog, rep from * to end.
Row 15: *k1, k2tog, rep from * to end (20 sts).
Row 16: p3tog, rep to last 2sts, p2tog.
Break off yarn, thread it through the remaining sts and fasten off securely.

Spikes (make 8):
Using yarn B, cast on 3 sts.
Row 1: k1, kfb, k1.
Row 2: and every alt row: P to end.
Row 3: k1, kfb, kfb, k1.
Row 5: k1, kfb, k2, kfb, k1.
Row 7: k1, kfb, k4, kfb, k1.
Row 9: k1, kfb, k6, kfb, k1.
Row 11: k1, kfb, k8, kfb, k1.

Row 13: k1, kfb, k10, kfb, k1.
Row 15: k1, kfb, k12, kfb, k1.
Row 17: k1, kfb, k14, kfb, k1.
Row 19: k1, kfb, k16, kfb, k1.
Row 20: p to end.
Cast off.

Earflaps (make 2):

Using yarn C, cast on 3 sts.
Work 20 rows as for spikes.
Row 21: k1, kfb, k18, kfb, k1.
Row 22: p to end.
Cont straight in st st until work measures
10cm/4in from cast on edge.
Cast off.

Spots (make 12 bobbles)

Using yarn C, cast on 1 st.
Row 1: Working all of the following into your cast
on stitch making sure you carry the yarn to the
back when knitting and to the front when purling
(k1, p1, k1, p1, k1, p1, k1, p1, k1), complete the
stitch, turn work and p9.
Row 2: k9
Row 3: p2tog x 2, p1, p2tog x 2.
Row 4: k2tog, k1, k2tog.
Row 5: Pass the second and third sts over the first
st and off the needle. Break off yarn, ensuring you
leave a long tail for attaching the spot to the hat,
and thread it through the remaining st.

Eyes (make 2):

Trace the template shown opposite onto card and
cut it out. Pin the template onto the white felt and
cut out the shape using pinking shears. Do this
twice – once for each eye.

Making up:

Sew the side edges of the hat using mattress
stitch (see page 22). This seam marks the centre-
back of the hat. Attach an earflap to each side
of hat, 14 sts away from the seam on either side,
using mattress stitch. Pair up spikes and overstitch
around. Attach the spikes to the seam of the hat.
Sew 6 bobbles onto each side of the hat. Position
a black button on each of the white felt circles,
using the picture opposite to guide you, then
sew them in place. Position the white circles on
the front of the hat, using the picture opposite to
guide you, then sew them to the hat.

Tassels:

Make 2 5cm/2in-long tassels (see page 38) using
yarn A. Attach 1 tassel to the end of each earflap.

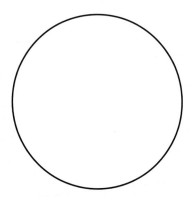

Template for eye

OWL HAT

Rachel Henderson

*Twit twoo! Make this loveable bobble-eared and
bright-eyed owl hat using cosy Cashsoft DK.*

Size: 6–10 years: 50cm/19½in
circumference

Materials:

~ Yarn A: 1 x 50g ball of Rowan
  Cashsoft DK shade 532, Vamp.
~ Yarn B: 1 x 50g ball of Rowan
  Cashsoft DK shade 509, Lime.
~ Scrap of white and blue dk
  yarn.
~ Stuffing or toy filling.
~ Orange felt
~ White card, pencil and paper
  scissors.

Hook:

~ 3.5mm (US 4/E) crochet hook.

Tension:

18dc and 18 rows to 10cm/4in
square.

Pattern:

Using yarn A, make 6ch and ss into first ch to form a ring.
Round 1: 12dc into ring (12 sts).
Round 2: [1dc into next st, 2dc into next st] rep around (18 sts).
Round 3: [1dc into next 2 sts, 2dc into next st] rep around (24 sts).
Round 4: [1dc into next 3 sts, 2dc into next st] rep around (30 sts).
Round 5: [1dc into next 4 sts, 2dc into next st] rep around (36 sts).
Round 6: [1dc into next 5 sts, 2dc into next st] rep around (42 sts).
Round 7: [1dc into next 6 sts, 2dc into next st] rep around (48 sts).
Round 8: [1dc into next 7 sts, 2dc into next st] rep around (54 sts).
Round 9: [1dc into next 8 sts, 2dc into next st] rep around (60 sts).
Round 10: [1dc into next 9 sts, 2dc into next st] rep around (66 sts)
Round 11: [1dc into next 10 sts, 2dc into next st] rep around (72 sts).
Row 12: [1dc into next 11 sts, 2dc into next st] rep around (78 sts).
Row 13: [1dc into next 12 sts, 2dc into next st] rep around (84 sts).
Row 14: [1dc into next 13 sts, 2dc into next st] rep around (92 sts).
Round 15: Miss 1dc, 1dc into every following st (91 sts).
Round 16: Miss 1dc, 1dc into every following st (90 sts).
Next few rounds: Work in dc on every round until work measures
17.5cm/6¾in.
Last 2 rounds: Change to yarn B, 1dc in each st around.

Eyes (make 2):
Using blue yarn, make 6ch, ss into first ch to form ring.
Round 1: ch1, 6dc into ring, ss into top of ch to join (6 st).
Round 2: Change to white yarn. ch1, 2dc into each dc around.
ss into top of ch to join (12 sts).
Round 3: ch1, [1dc into next st, 2 dc into next st], rep around, ss
into top of ch to join (18 sts).
Round 4: ch1, [1dc into next 2 sts, 2 dc into next st], rep around,
ss into top of ch to join (24 sts).

Round 5: ch1, [1dc into next 3 sts, 2 dc into next st], rep around, ss into top of ch to join (30 sts).
Round 6: ch1, [1dc into next 4 sts, 2 dc into next st], rep around, ss into top of ch to join (36 sts).
Fasten off securely.

Ears (make 2):
Using yarn A, make 25ch, ss into first ch from hook.
Rounds 1–3: 1dc in each st around.
Next few rounds: [1dc, dec1] rep until 1 st remains.
Fasten off securely.

Bobble (make 2):
Using yarn B, make 6ch, ss into first ch to form ring.
Round 1: Using yarn B, ch1, 6dc into ring (6 sts).
Round 2: [1dc into next st, 2dc into next st] rep around (9 sts).
Round 3: [1dc into next 2 sts, 2dc into next st] rep around (12 sts).
Rounds 4–6: 1 dc into each st around.
Round 7: [dec1, 1dc] rep around (8 sts).
Next few rounds: [dec 1] until 1 st is left.
Fasten off securely.

Beak
Trace the template shown opposite onto white card and cut it out. Pin it onto the orange felt, draw around the template and cut out the beak shape.

Making up
Position the eyes on the centre-front of hat using the photograph opposite to guide you, then attach them to the hat with yarn B using a blanket stitch (see page 37).

Stuff the ears with toy filling. Sew up both ears using mattress stitch (see page 22). Position the ears on the hat using the photograph opposite to guide you, then attach them to the hat using an overstitch. Position the beak on the hat using the photograph opposite to guide you, then attach it to the hat. Attach 1 bobble to the tip of each ear.

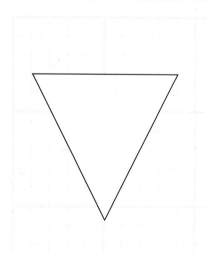

Template for beak

CROCHETED WOLF HAT

Rachel Henderson

This project has been crocheted using gorgeous Rowan Pure Wool yarn. To create the effect of a wolf's fur, a crocheted fur stitch is used, and all the loops are brushed out to make the hat nice and hairy!

Size: 6–10 years: 50cm/19½in circumference

Materials:

~ Yarn A: 1 x 50g ball of Rowan Pure Wool DK shade 002, Shale.
~ Yarn B: 1 x 50g ball of Rowan Pure Wool DK shade 013, Enamel.
~ 2 x small black buttons.

Hook:

~ Size 3.5mm (US 4E) crochet hook.

Tension:

18htr and 13rows to 10cm/4in square

Abbreviations:

Lp1: Insert the hook into the corresponding st on the previous row. Take the hook over the working yarn and hook it both behind and in front of the index finger. Pull the 2 loops of yarn through, releasing the long loop over the finger to lie at the back of the work. Take the yarn over the hook once more and pull it through to complete the stitch.

Pattern:

Using yarn A, make 6ch and ss into first ch to form ring.
Round 1: 12dc into ring (12 sts).
Round 2: [1htr into next st, 2htr into next st] rep around (18 sts).
Round 3: [1htr into next 2 sts, 2htr into next st] rep around (24 sts).
Round 4: [1htr into next 3 sts, 2htr into next st] rep around (30 sts).
Round 5: [1htr into next 4 sts, 2htr into next st] rep around (36 sts).
Round 6: [1htr into next 5 sts, 2htr into next st] rep around (42 sts).
Round 7: [1htr into next 6 sts, 2htr into next st] rep around (48 sts).
Round 8: [1htr into next 7 sts, 2htr into next st] rep around (54 sts).
Round 9: [1htr into next 8 sts, 2htr into next st] rep around (60 sts).
Round 10: [1htr into next 9 sts, 2htr into next st] rep around (66 sts).
Round 11: [1htr into next 10 sts, 2htr into next st] rep around (72 sts).
Round 12: [1htr into next 1 sts, 2htr into next st] rep around (78 sts).
Round 13: Miss 1htr, 1htr into every following st (77 sts).
Round 14: Miss 1htr, 1htr into every following st (76 sts).
Round 15: Change to yarn B. [1dc, lp 1], rep around.
Rounds 16 & 17: dc into each st around.
Round 18: [1dc, lp 1], rep around.
Repeat rounds 15–17 4 more times.
Last round: dc in each st around.
Fasten off securely.

Earflaps:

Using yarn A, starting 8 sts in from the centre (both sides) at the bottom of the hat, work 1dc in each of the next 20 sts.
Foundation row: ch1, 1dc in each of the next 20dc
Row 1: ch1, 1dc, dec1, dc across to last 3 sts, dec1, 1dc (18 sts).
Row 2: ch1, 1dc in each st across.
Row 3: ch1, 1dc, dec1, dc across to last 3 sts, dec1, 1dc (16 sts).

Row 4: ch1, 1dc in each st across.
Row 5: ch1, 1dc, dec1, dc across to last 3 sts, dec1, 1dc (14 sts).
Row 6: ch1, 1dc in each st across.
Row 7: ch1, 1dc, dec1, dc across to last 3 sts, dec1, 1dc (12 sts).
Row 8: ch1, 1dc in each st across.
Row 9: ch1, 1dc, dec1, dc across to last 3 sts, dec1, 1dc (10 sts).
Row 10: ch1, 1dc in each st across.
Row 11: ch1, 1dc, dec1, dc across to last 3 sts, dec1, 1dc (8 sts).
Row 12: ch1, 1dc in each st across.
Row 13: ch1, 1dc, dec1, dc across to last 3 sts, dec1, 1dc (6 sts).
Row 14: ch1, 1dc in each st across.
Row 15: ch1, [dec1] x 3 (3 sts).
Row 16: ch1, 1dc, dec1 (2 sts).
Row 17: dec1 (1 st).
Fasten off securely.

Outer ear (make 2):
Using yarn A, make 16ch.
Foundation row: ch1, 1dc in each st across.
Row 1: ch1, 1dc, dec1, dc across to last 3 sts, dec1, 1dc (14 sts).
Row 2: ch1, 1dc in each st across.
Row 3: ch1, 1dc, dec1, dc across to last 3 sts, dec1, 1dc (12 sts).
Row 4: ch1, 1dc in each st across.
Row 5: ch1, 1dc, dec1, dc across to last 3 sts, dec1, 1dc (10 sts).
Row 6: ch1, 1dc in each st across.
Row 7: ch1, 1dc, dec1, dc across to last 3 sts, dec1, 1dc (8 sts).
Row 8: ch1, 1dc in each st across.
Row 9: ch1, 1dc, dec1, dc across to last 3 sts, dec1, 1dc (6 sts).
Row 10: ch1, 1dc in each st across.
Row 11: ch1, 1dc, [dec1] x 2, dc1 (4 sts).
Row 12: ch1, 1dc in each st across.
Row 13: ch1, dec1 x 2 (2 sts).
Row 14: dec1 (1 st).
Fasten off securely.

Inside ear (make 2):
Using yarn B, make 10ch.
Foundation row: ch1, dc in each st across.
Row 1: ch1, [1dc, lp1], rep across.
Row 2: ch1, 1dc, dec1, dc across to last 3 sts, dec1, 1dc (8 sts).
Row 3: ch1, [1dc, lp1], rep across.

Row 4: ch1, 1dc, dec1, dc across to last sts, dec1, 1dc (6 sts).
Row 5: ch1, [1dc, lp1], rep across.
Row 6: ch1, [dec1] x 2, 1dc (4 sts).
Row 7: ch1, [1dc, lp1] x 2.
Row 8: dec1 x 2 (2 sts).
Fasten off securely.

Eyes (make 2):

Using yarn B, make 2ch.
Foundation row: Work 4 dcs into 2nd ch (4 sts).
Row 1: 2dc into each st across (8 sts).
Row 2: dc into each st across.
Row 3: 2dc into each st across (16 sts).
Row 4: dc into each st across.
Fasten off securely.

Mouth:

Using yarn A, make 4ch and ss into first ch to form ring.
Round 1: ch1, 6dc into ring, ss into ch to join (6 sts).
Round 2: ch1, 2dc into each st around, ss into ch to join (12 sts).
Round 3: ch1, [1dc into next st, 2dc into next st], rep around, ss into ch to join (18 sts).
Round 4: ch1, [1dc into next 2 sts, 2dc into next st], rep around, ss into ch to join (24sts).
Round 5: ch1, [1dc into next 3 sts, 2dc into next st], rep around, ss into ch to join (30 sts).
Round 6: ch1, [2dc into next st, 1dc into next 14 sts] x 2, ss into ch to join (32 sts).
Fasten off securely.

Making up:

Cut open all the loops created and brush out the yarn. Position the crocheted mouth and eyes using the photograph opposite to guide you, then attach them to the hat using an overstitch. Stitch a black button to the centre of each eye using yarn B. Embroider the nose and mouth using the picture opposite to guide you, using backstitch and satin stitch (see page 37). Embroider whiskers using a French knot stitch (see page 99). Attach 1 inner-ear piece to the front of 2 outer-ear pieces. Repeat with the other ear pieces. Pair up both ears, overstitch around and attach to top centre of hat.

CROCHETED MONKEY HAT

Susan Urquhart

This is a really fun project to make. By crocheting a big mouth, eyes and some stick out ears you can create a cheeky wee monkey hat!

Size: 6–10 years: 50cm/19½in circumference

Materials:

~ Yarn A: 2 x 50g balls of Rowan Pima Cotton shade 073, Bark.
~ Yarn B: 1 x 50g ball of Rowan Pima Cotton shade 071, Dijon.
~ Yarn C: 1 x 50g ball of Rowan Pima Cotton shade 050, Pampas.
~ Yarn D: 1 x 50g ball of Rowan Pima Cotton shade 074, Verdigris.
~ Yarn E: 1 x 50g ball of Rowan Pure Wool DK shade 002, Shale.
~ Scrap of red dk yarn.
~ Stuffing or toy filling.
~ 2 x black buttons.

Crochet hook:

~ Size 3.5mm (US 4E) crochet hook

Tension:

18dc and 18 rows to 10cm/4in square.

Pattern:

Using yarn A, follow the same pattern as Owl Hat (see p.127).
After Round 16: Work in dc on every round until hat measures 19cm/7½in. Fasten off securely.

Earflaps (make 2):

Using yarn A, and starting 13 sts along (both sides) from bottom centre st, work 1dc in each of next 17 sts.
Row 1: ch1, 1dc in each of the next 17sts.
Row 2: ch1, 1dc, dec1, dc across to last 3 sts, dec1, 1dc (15 sts).
Row 3: ch1, 1dc in each st across.
Row 4: ch1, 1dc, dec1, dc across to last 3 sts, dec1, 1dc (13 sts).
Row 5: ch1, 1dc in each st across.
Row 6: ch1, 1dc, dec1, dc across to last 3 sts, dec1, 1dc (11 sts).
Row 7: ch1, 1dc in each st across.
Row 8: ch1, 1dc, dec1, dc across to last 3 sts, dec1, 1dc (9 sts).
Row 9: ch1, 1dc in each st across.
Row 10: ch1, 1dc, dec1, dc across to last 3 sts, dec1, 1dc (7 sts).
Row 11: ch1, 1dc in each st across.
Row 12: ch1, 1dc, [dec1] x 3 (4 sts).
Row 13: ch1, [dec 1] x 2 (2 sts).
Fasten off securely.

Cords (make 2):

Using yarn A, ch50.
Dc into 2nd ch from hook, 1dc in each st to end.
Fasten off securely.

Ears (make 4):

Using yarn A, ch 6 sts and join with ss to form ring.
Round 1: ch3 (counts as first tr), 11tr into ring, ss into third of 3ch, pull tail to close ring (12 sts).

Round 2: ch3 (counts as first tr), work 1tr into same st as ch3, 2tr into each st around, ss into third of 3ch (24 sts).

Round 3: ch3 (counts as first tr), work 1tr into same st as ch3, 2tr into each st around, ss into third of 3ch (48 sts).

Inner ear (make 2):

Using yarn E, ch 6sts and join with ss to form ring.

Round 1: ch3 (counts as first tr), 11tr into ring, ss into third of 3ch, pull tail to close ring (12 sts).

Round 2: ch3 (counts as first tr), work 1tr into same st as ch3, 2tr into each st around, ss into third of 3ch (24 sts).

Fasten off securely.

Outer eyes (make 2):

Using yarn E, follow the instructions for the inner ear.

Inner eyes (make 2):

Using yarn C (cream) ch 6sts and join with ss to form ring.

Round 1: ch3 (counts as first tr), 11tr into circle, ss into third of 3ch, pull tail to close ring (12 sts).

Fasten off securely.

Upper mouth (make 2):

Using yarn E, ch16.

Row 1: dc into each st across.

Row 2: 1dc, dec1, dc to last 3 sts, dec1, 1dc (14 sts).

Row 3: dc into each st across.

Row 4: 1dc, dec1, dc to last 3 sts, dec1, 1dc (12 sts).

Row 5: dc into each st across.

Row 6: 1dc, dec1, dc to last 3 sts, dec1, 1dc (10 sts).

Row 7: dc into each st across.

Row 8: 1dc, dec1, dc to last 3 sts, dec1, 1dc (8 sts).

Row 9: dc into each st across.

Row 10: 1dc, dec1, dc to last 3 sts, dec1, 1dc (6 sts).

Row 11: dc into each st across.

Row 12: 1dc, [dec1] x 2, 1dc (4 sts).

Row 13: [dec1] x 2. (2 sts).

Fasten off securely.

Lower mouth (make 2):

Using yarn E, ch20.

Row 1: dc into each st across.

Row 2: 1dc, dec1, dc to last 3 sts, dec1, 1dc (18 sts).

Row 3: dc into each st across.

Row 4: 1dc, dec1, dc to last 3 sts, dec1, 1dc (16 sts).

Row 5: dc into each st across.

Row 6: 1dc, dec1, dc to last 3 sts, dec1, 1dc (14 sts).

Row 7: dc into each st across.

Row 8: 1dc, dec1, dc to last 3 sts, dec1, 1dc (12 sts).

Row 9: dc into each st across.

Row 10: 1dc, dec1, dc to last 3 sts, dec1, 1dc (10 sts).

Row 11: dc into each st across.

Row 12: 1dc, dec1, dc to last 3 sts, dec1, 1dc (8 sts).

Row 13: dc into each st across.

Row 14: 1dc, dec1, dc to last 3 sts, dec1, 1dc (6 sts).

Row 15: 1dc, [dec1] x 2, 1dc (4 sts).

Fasten off securely.

Tongue:

Using scrap red DK yarn, ch10.

Row 1–10: dc into each st across.

Row 11: 1dc, dec1, dc to last 3 sts, dec1, 1dc (8 sts).

Row 12: 1dc, dec1, dc to last 3 sts, dec1, 1dc (6 sts).

Row 13: 1dc, [dec1] x 2, 1dc (4 sts).

Row 14: [dec1] x 2 (2 sts).

Fasten off securely.

Large banana skin:

Using yarn D, ch6.

Rows 1–3: ch3, 1tr into each st across (6 sts).

Change to yarn B.

Row 1: ch 3, work 2tr into each st across (12 sts).

Row 2: ch 3 [1tr in next st, 2tr in next st], rep to end (18 sts).

Rows 3–6: ch 3, 1tr in each st across.

First peel:

Row 7: ch 3, 1tr in each of next 5 sts (top of ch3 counts as 1st st), turn (6 sts).

Rows 8–28: ch 3, 1tr in each st.

Row 29: ss2tog, 1dc in each of next 2 sts, ss2tog (4 sts).

Row 30: 1dc in each st.
Row 31: [ss2tog] x 2 (2 sts).
Row 32: ss2tog (1 st).
Fasten off securely.
Second and third peels:
With RS facing, join yarn B at the base of the first peel and ss 6 sts.
Work as rows 7–33 of first peel.
Rep at base of 2nd peel for 3rd peel.

Small banana skin (make 2):

Using yarn D, ch3.
Row 1: 1dc in 2nd st from hook, 1dc in next st (2 sts).
Rows 2–3: ch 1, 1dc in each st (2 sts).
Change to yarn B.
Row 1: ch1, 3dc in each st across (6 sts).
Row 2: ch1, 2dc in each st across (12 sts).
Row 3: ch1 [1dc in next st, 2dc in next st] repeat across (18 sts).
Rows 4–7: ch 1 1dc in each st.
First peel:
Row 8: ch 1, 1dc in each of next 6 sts, turn (6 sts).
Rows 9–29: 1dc in each st.
Row 30: ss2tog, 1dc in next 2sts, ss2tog (4 sts).
Row 31: 1dc in each st.
Row 32: [ss2tog] x 2 (2 sts).
Row 33: ss2tog (1 st).
Fasten off securely.
Second and third peels:
With RS facing, join yarn B at the base of the first peel and ss 6 sts.
Work as rows 8–33 of first peel.
Rep at base of second peel for third peel.

Banana (make 2):

Using yarn C ch 6 sts and join with ss to form ring.
Round 1: ch1, work 15dc into circle, ss into ch1, pull circle to ring (15 sts).
Continue and work 1dc into each st around until work measures 10cm/4in.
Fasten off securely.

Making up:

Stuff the top of the large banana skin with toy filling. Position it on the hat using the picture as a guide, then sew it in place. To make the ears, sew 1 small grey circle onto 1 large brown circle. With WS facing in, sew 2 large brown circles together, leaving a small gap. Turn the RS out and stuff with toy filling. Position the ears on the hat using the pictures to guide you, then stitch them onto the hat. Repeat with the other ear pieces.

To make the mouth, align the upper-mouth pieces with their RS facing in and sew together, leaving a small gap. Turn the RS out and fill with stuffing. Embroider the nose using back stitch (see page 37) and stitch a centre line through both layers. Align the lower-mouth pieces with their RS facing in and sew together, leaving a small gap. Turn the RS out and fill with stuffing. Position the mouth pieces on the hat using the pictures to guide you, then sew them onto hat. Sew the tongue onto the mouth.

To make the eyes, position the large grey pieces above the mouth using the pictures to guide you, then sew them onto the hat. Sew the small inner eyes on top, then add a black button. Repeat with the other mouth pieces. Sew up the top part of each banana skin and attach onto the end of each chain. Stuff both bananas, then attach them to the inside of the banana skins.

RECYCLED MEERHAT & MATCHING GLOVES

Karen Masters

It's a sad occasion when you find a hole in a favourite woollen jumper. But don't worry - give it a new lease of life as a cute animal hat! This is a fun, simple and quick way to make a cheeky meerkat hat with matching paw mittens.

Size: Child/adult (one size).

Materials needed:

~ Old woollen jumper
~ Grey felt for eyes
~ White card, paper scissors and pencil.
~ Tailor's chalk.
~ Fabric scissors.
~ 25g wool tops in brown, white, black, orange and gold.
~ Clover felting punch tool and mat.
~ Sewing machine.
~ Brown cotton thread.

Using a clover felting punch tool and mat: A clover tool contains 5 felting needles that each have small barbs on the end. These special barbs enable you to push loose wool through to the back of a woven surface (which is placed onto a clover mat). The process felts the 2 sets of fibres together, which permanently attaches them to each other. The technique can be used to create interesting appliqué wool designs.

Pattern:

Hat:

Step 1: Using the pattern diagram on page 141, create a card pattern piece for the main hat using the dimensions provided. Position the hat template on the front of the jumper (if your jumper has a ribbed edge, position the card pattern as suggested on the hat diagram) and trace the outline using tailor's chalk. Cut out the shape. Repeat on the back of the jumper.

Step 2: Trace the template provided for the ears and eyes onto card and cut out. For the ears, place the template onto the jumper, trace twice using tailor's chalk and cut out the pieces. For the eyes, place the template onto grey felt, trace twice using tailor's chalk and cut out.

Step 3: Position the eye and ear pieces using the picture opposite to guide you. If an eye or ear is slightly squint, don't worry – it just adds to the character of the meerhat.

Step 4: Embellish around the edges of the ear pieces with a twisted piece of wool tops using a clover punch tool and mat. Use the picture opposite to guide you. This will create a tufted look and prevent the jumper fabric from fraying.

Step 5: Embellish around the edges of the eyes with large twists of brown wool tops and a small tuft of orange wool tops using the clover punch tool and mat and the picture opposite to guide you. Create a small ball of black tops to make an eyeball for each eye, and highlight each eyeball by needle-punching in a small piece of white tops.

Step 6: Place the eyes in position on the front piece of the hat (using the diagram opposite to guide you) and punch across the whole of each eye (edges and centre) with your clover tool until secure.

Step 7: Make a larger twisted piece of black wool tops for the nose and punch into the centre, using the diagram opposite as a guide. Cut out a smiley mouth shape from the leftover jumper fabric and needle-punch this into place under wool nose.

Step 8: Place the 2 head pieces together with their RS facing inwards and, leaving a 1cm seam allowance, stitch around both sides of the hat using a sewing machine. Position the ears on either side of the head, using the photos to guide you, and hand stitch them into place using an overstitch.

The paws:
These are made from the sleeves of the jumper.
Step 1: Place your hand inside the cuff of the jumper sleeve so that the ribbed end of the sleeve sits on your wrist where you would like the ribbed cuff of your mittens to be. Measure the length of fabric required to make a mitten – include the fabric from the cuff wrist to about 20cm/8in beyond the longest finger. Cut straight across the sleeve beyond the height of the longest finger to cut off the fabric you need for 1 mitten. Lay this cut piece of sleeve over the other sleeve and use it as a template for cutting the fabric for the second mitten.

Step 2: Using small twists of black wool tops and the clover punch tool, embellish the top layer of each mitten with three claws to create finger divisions.

Step 3: To create the shape of the paws, use the photos to guide you and draw the shape of the paw onto the jumper fabric with tailor's chalk. Then turn the length of sleeve inside out and stitch around the outside (leaving a 1cm seam allowance), leaving the bottom, ribbed section open. Repeat with the fabric for the other hand.

Pattern Diagram & Template

Pattern: Main hat
Template: Eye and ear

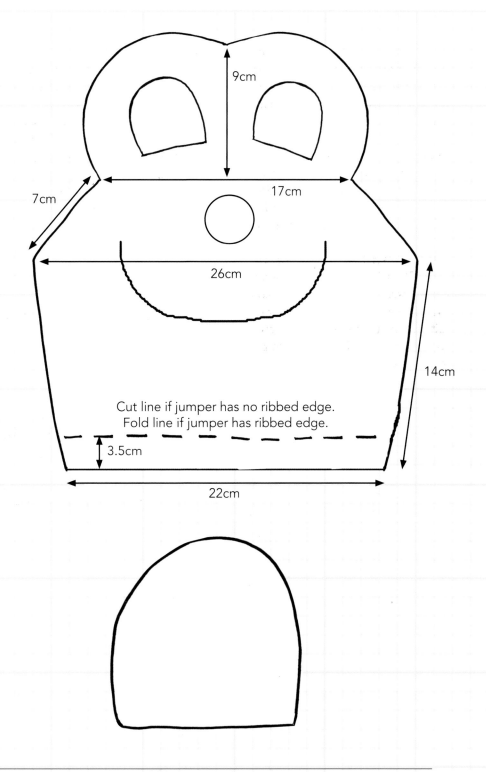

9cm

7cm

17cm

26cm

14cm

Cut line if jumper has no ribbed edge.
Fold line if jumper has ribbed edge.

3.5cm

22cm

Index

Acknowledgements

I feel so privileged to have been commissioned to write this book. It has been, without doubt, the most fun and enjoyable project I have ever worked on in the whole of my career as a freelance designer. I would like to say a big, big thank you to Kyle and Judith at Kyle Books for getting me involved, my lovely editor Catharine for helping me along the way, my two brilliant pattern checkers Eva and Sarah for doing such a fantastic job, Turnbull Grey for creating such a colourful and trendy-looking publication, Will Heap for the amazing photography and let's not forget all of the gorgeous models, especially those little cuties!! I would also like to say a big thanks to all my very talented contributors – Sarah, Helen, Susan, Charlotte, Ben and Karen, whose hats made me smile a lot!

My final thanks goes to my mum, dad and partner Andy, whose constant support and enthusiasm give me the confidence and motivation to keep designing, making and doing what I love.

The publishers and the author would like to thanks Rowan Yarns for sponsoring the projects. www.knitrowan.com